T0330653

Auditing Teams

The recent audit failures which have rocked financial markets worldwide have accentuated the need for a better understanding of the link between risk, control and audit quality; as well as emphasising the need to open the "black box" of the ways auditing firms actually function. Reflecting these imperatives, *Auditing Teams* unravels the organizational and management issues in audit firms that are key to achieving effectiveness in service provision.

Specifically, this key research reflects upon the relevance and dynamics of auditing teams and their impact on auditing quality, and specifically responding to the recent claim from regulators which highlights auditing team characteristics as the source of wide variations in quality.

By leveraging different perspectives – auditing, management accounting, organization and psychology – to investigate auditing teams and basing on evidence collected from the professional world, this book will provide a unique insight into the role of auditing teams on audit quality.

It will be of great interest to scholars and advanced students in auditing, as well as to practitioners and regulators in the field.

Mara Cameran, PhD, is researcher of accounting at Università Bocconi and professor of SDA at the Bocconi School of Management in Milan, Italy. She is an Italian CPA (Dottore Commercialista) and chartered auditor (Revisore Contabile), a member of the European Auditing Research Network (EARNet) scientific committee, and the European Accounting Association representative in the Consultative Advisory Group (CAG) of the International Accounting Education Standards Board (IAESB).

Angelo Ditillo, PhD, is associate professor of management accounting and control at Università Bocconi and professor of SDA Bocconi School of Management, Milan, Italy. He has been a visiting professor in many different institutions, including the Saïd Business School at the University of Oxford, the Iese Business School and the ESADE Business School in Spain, the University of Technology in Sydney, Australia, and the University of Paris, Dauphine.

Angela Pettinicchio, PhD, is assistant professor and instructor of financial reporting and International Accounting at Università Bocconi in Milan, Italy. She is a faculty member of the Accounting, Control, Corporate and Real Estate Finance Department and coordinator of the Financial Frauds Area of the Osservatorio di Revisione (Audit Research Center) at the SDA Bocconi School of Management in Milan.

Routledge Focus on Business and Management

The fields of business and management have grown exponentially as areas of research and education. This growth presents challenges for readers trying to keep up with the latest important insights. Routledge Focus on Business and Management presents small books on big topics and how they intersect with the world of business.

Individually, each title in the series provides coverage of a key academic topic, whilst collectively, the series forms a comprehensive collection across the business disciplines.

Auditing Teams
Dynamics and Efficiency

**Mara Cameran, Angelo Ditillo and
Angela Pettinicchio**

LONDON AND NEW YORK

First published 2017
by Routledge
2 Park Square, Milton Park, Abingdon, Oxon OX14 4RN

and by Routledge
605 Third Avenue, New York, NY 10017

*Routledge is an imprint of the Taylor & Francis Group, an informa
business*

British Library Cataloguing-in-Publication Data
A catalogue record for this book is available from the British
Library

Library of Congress Cataloging-in-Publication Data
Names: Cameran, Mara, 1970– author. | Pettinicchio, Angela,
    1981– author. | Ditillo, Angelo, 1970– author.
Title: Auditing teams : dynamics and efficiency / Mara Cameran,
    Angela Pettinicchio, Angelo Ditillo.
Description: 1 Edition. | New York : Routledge, 2017. |
    Includes bibliographical references and index.
Identifiers: LCCN 2016056822 (print) | LCCN 2016057627
    (ebook) | ISBN 9781138682702 (hardback : alk. paper) |
    ISBN 9781315544953 (ebk) | ISBN 9781315544953 (eBook)
Subjects: LCSH: Auditing. | Teams in the workplace.
Classification: LCC HF5667. C256 2017 (print) | LCC HF5667
    (ebook) | DDC 657/.45—dc23
LC record available at https://lccn.loc.gov/2016056822

ISBN: 978-1-138-68270-2 (hbk)

Typeset in Times New Roman
by Apex CoVantage, LLC

To our sons Claudio, Daniele, Emilio and Gioele, who every day remind us about the beauty of curiosity

Contents

1 Introduction

The audit failures that have shocked financial markets worldwide have accentuated the need for opening the "black box" of auditing firms' functioning. With this premise, this book has the objective to explore the audit firms' organizational and management issues that are key to achieve effectiveness in auditing service provision. More specifically, starting from acknowledging the knowledge-intensive nature of audit firms and illustrating the relevant characteristics of individual auditors, this work aims to reflect upon the relevance and dynamics of auditing teams and their impact on auditing quality. Our work represents a response to the recent claim from regulators that consider audit team characteristics as particularly important:

> Based on more than ten years of oversight, the Board knows that, even within a single firm and notwithstanding firm-wide or network-wide quality control systems, the quality of individual audit engagements varies. PCAOB inspectors have observed a wide variation in the quality of auditing by many engagement teams.
>
> (PCAOB 2013: 6)

An important distinctive element of our contribution is that it leverages on different disciplines (psychology, organization, auditing and management accounting) to investigate audit teams, and we complement our arguments with evidence collected from the professional world.

In our book, we examine the specific features of audit teams as well as their dynamics, which matter in terms of the final performance they are able to achieve. In particular, we analyze the impact of group characteristics, the interaction between individuals, and the corresponding forms of control adopted at the team level on audit quality. In fact, individual auditors do not operate in isolation and their behaviour depends on the dynamics activated within the audit teams in which they work.

These aspects could be of interest for both the academic and professional audiences. Therefore, our work is oriented to not only researchers in the fields of auditing and management accounting but also to practitioners operating in the audit and other professional firms as well as managers of auditees involved in the audit process.

The book is structured in six additional chapters after this one. The objective of the second chapter is to analyze auditing firms as professional service firms and describe their specifics. This type of firm combines a high degree of interaction with the client, together with a high degree of customization. For this reason, professional service firms compete simultaneously in two markets: the "output" market for the services, and the "input" market for the professional workforce. The aim of the chapter is to illustrate how auditing firms find balance between the conflicting demands and constraints of these two markets that constitutes the special challenge for the management of the professional service firms. This equilibrium is maintained through the firm's economic and organizational structures as well as through the use of suitable management control mechanisms. These would allow, on the one hand, to achieve an appropriate balance between controlling audit costs and maintaining a high level of quality and on the other hand to prevent behaviours that can negatively affect audit quality. A description of these aspects as well as of the major variables that may affect their interaction will be provided and discussed.

The third chapter is focused on individual auditors. Regulators and professional bodies around the world are aware of the importance of auditors' individual characteristics and set different requirements that people should meet in order to become certified auditors. All the above is in the spirit of serving the public interest by contributing to the ability of the auditing profession to meet the needs of the persons who rely on the opinion expressed in the audit reports. Also auditing firms consider people selection as one of their key processes. From an academic point of view, different contributors have questioned whether there are differences in individual auditor judgements and outcomes and what are the relevant individual characteristics for explaining these differences. A summary of this research is presented in the chapter. The literature implicitly assumes that the quality of the audit being undertaken by a team depends on the sum of the skills and personality of individuals. However, individual auditors do not work in isolation and are affected by the interaction within the audit teams in which they operate.

In Chapter 4 the literature on audit team composition and its effect on audit activity is presented, followed by an analysis of the literature on audit team dynamics, such as brainstorming and consultations within the firms. This chapter is complemented by a focus on professional practice and regulatory standards about audit teams. Reference will be made to audit standards and to professional practice via information disclosed in audit firms' transparency reports, audit quality reports, and annual reviews.

Chapter 5 concentrates on the forms of control, including auditing quality controls and clan controls, adopted by auditing firms at the team level and the importance of communication in socializing auditing staff, relevant to enhancing the auditing teams' level of performance. In addition, it illustrates the potential quality threatening behaviours that can be activated within the teams, as well as their potential determinants and consequences.

The aim of Chapter 6 is to report the voice of practitioners involved in the audit process, mainly collected by means of interviews. In particular, the chapter reports evidence from respondents with different roles within the Big 4 in relation to the following aspects: audit team composition and related criteria and policies to select the members of the teams; team dynamics and internal organization and management of the team; finally, team performance measurement and control as well as how team members are rewarded.

The last chapter draws from the arguments presented in the previous chapters, illustrating the main conclusions and providing the main implications of our contribution.

Reference

Public Company Accounting Oversight Board (PCAOB). (2013). Release No. 2013–009. Improving the transparency of audits: proposed amendments to PCAOB auditing standards to provide disclosure in the auditor's report of certain participants in the audit. Retrieved from http://www.ey.com/publication/vwluassetsdld/pcaobproposal_transparency_4december2013/$file/pcaob proposal_transparency_4december2013.pdf?OpenElement

2 The management of auditing firms

Introduction

Auditing firms are categorized in the management literature as professional and knowledge-intensive firms (Ekstedt 1989; Starbuck 1992; Winch and Schneider 1993; Von Nordenflycht 2010). Therefore, the characteristics assigned to these categories of firms can be extended to the auditing firms, and are useful to understand their functioning. Auditing firms are professional service organizations, because their experts belong to a recognized profession (Von Nordenflycht 2010). A profession possesses at least four characteristics apart from expertise: an ethical code, cohesion, collegial enforcement of standards and autonomy (Schriesheim, Von Glinow, and Kerr 1977). Ethical codes require that professionals operate impersonally. They work as third parties to transactions and act on behalf of the various stakeholders that are interested in company accounts. To play this role they need to be independent and perceived as disinterested subjects. Professionals identify strongly with their professions; they not only follow the professional standards, but also they are convinced that only those that belong to the profession have the right competencies and ethics to enforce those standards (Starbuck 1992; Winch and Schneider 1993; Von Nordenflycht 2010). Auditing firms are also knowledge-intensive organizations. This is because they employ people in areas that require specific expertise. So their capital consists mainly of human capital even if part of the knowledge is institutionalized and localized in the organization as collective frames of reference, systematized methods of work and sophisticated routines (Ekstedt 1989; Starbuck 1992; Winch and Schneider 1993; Ditillo 2004).

The above elements have implications in terms of how auditing firms are organized and managed. First, in the design of these firms, the number of hierarchical levels is limited because coordination and control are achieved directly by professionals. Second, there is a constant tension between professional and organizational norms (Hinings, Brown, and Greenwood 1991). Third, there is a need to manage properly complex interpersonal dynamics inherent in the development and dissemination of knowledge within the firm and to define knowledge management strategies which influence the way in which the professionals operate within the firm (Morris and Empson 1998). Finally, in order to assess where and how value is generated, specific performance metrics are needed and are aimed at highlighting the productivity of people (Barber and Strack 2005). Much attention is focused on the time of professionals. The billed time ratio, which is the ratio of hours billed to total professional hours supplied, is monitored carefully. In addition, if it is necessary to employ idle time or for marketing reasons some engagements are billed at lower rates, the resulting variance is subject to close scrutiny (Anthony and Govindarajan 2007).

The management of auditing firms

Auditing firms operate in two different markets at the same time. On the one hand, they operate in the market of the services they provide. On the other hand, they act in the market for professional workforce. Balancing the tension between these two markets is achieved by means of the firm's economic and organizational structures (Maister 1982). According to Maister (1982) the management of professional service firms requires the consideration of the various links that connect the two markets and the two structures.

* *The market for professional labour.* Professional service firms organize career paths along the three levels of partners, managers, and junior staff described previously. New entrants start at the bottom and progress through the organization. Two elements are particularly important in the functioning of this market: the normal amount of time necessary for being promoted and the proportion promoted. Auditors that are not promoted in what is considered a reasonable amount of time will either decide to leave the company or alternatively will be suggested to do so by those who do not think they are promotable (Maister 1982).
* *The market for the firm's services.* This market has already been taken into consideration in relation to the link with the firm's economic structure (by means of the billing rates) and with the organizational structure (by means of the project team structure). One key element that links this market to the market for professionals is represented by the quality of professional labour that the firm would like to hire and attract. Top professionals will be attracted by those firms that show that the projects in which they engage are challenging and those that provide major chances for professional achievements and developments (Maister 1982).
* *The organizational structure.* The structure's key feature is that the national office of a firm is governed through a form of representative

democracy. At the top there is a partnership body, which elects an executive policy committee. This latter typically represents major functional areas. Other committees are concerned with both major functional areas and managerial functions such as professional development, professional standards and marketing. One important element is that in the national offices there are committees of partners drawn from the field. In addition, employments at the national or international offices are often temporary appointments. National partners and national executive partners usually go back to the local offices after a predefined period of time. Moreover, most professionals aspire to partnership and most partners operate at the local office level. The reference for the activity and commitment is at the local and not the national office (Greenwood, Hinings, and Brown 1990). Normally, these firms are organized in three different levels. At the top are owner-partners who are in charge of managing the relationships with the clients and the policy and strategic orientation of the firm. At an intermediate level are the managers who are in charge of dealing with the day-to-day interaction with the clients and monitor the activities of the junior staff. At the lowest level are the junior staff who carry out the operating activities and some supervisory tasks (Maister 1982, 1993; Hinings, Brown, and Greenwood 1991). Because of their customized nature, the activities of the auditing firms are organized by combining members of the three levels described earlier in teams (Maister 1982; Anthony and Govindarajan 2007). These latter allow to combine the specialist knowledge of many individuals and to achieve effective integration while reducing the need of knowledge transfer through cross-learning by team members (Ditillo 2004). This means that junior staff collaborate with more senior auditors, and also that a rather clear-cut division of labour, both vertically and horizontally, is activated. Teams are organized in a way that allows members to have a clear idea of their own contributions (Kärreman and Alvesson 2004).

- *The economic structure.* Revenue generation in auditing firms is the result of the relative hours provided to the customers by the different levels of auditors in the hierarchical pyramid as well as of the various billing rates – the hourly charge to clients for the services provided by the different auditors. Cost occurrence is related to the remuneration assigned to the different auditors' groups. One essential element in explaining the performance of auditing firms is related to the fact that the relative revenue generation levels do not correspond to the relative compensation levels. This imbalance is essential to understand the financial achievements of auditing firms. This means that the compensation of partners derives only partially from the high rates that partners can charge their clients. Partners' rewards are to a large extent the result of the ability of the firm, by means of its project team structure, to leverage the professional knowledge of the seniors with the contribution of the juniors to satisfy clients' needs (Maister 1982).

The management of professional service firms requires to achieve a balance between the previously described markets and structures. The firm cannot introduce changes in one of these elements neglecting the implications that these changes have on the other elements. Although many firms concentrate their attention on the design of their organizational and economic structures, these analyses must be carried out by integrating them with the market for the firm's services and that of professional labour forces (Maister 1982, 1993).

The management control in auditing firms

Auditors have to put a reasonable level of competencies, concentration, and attention in carrying out their work. To this end, auditing standards and guidelines suggest principles and procedures to achieve this level and also require auditors to plan and control their activities effectively. High professional standards alone, however, are not enough to guarantee the outcomes of auditing firms and their durability. Long-term success is also the result of the implementation of effective management controls (Otley and Pierce 1996; Sweeney and Pierce 2004; Pierce and Sweeney 2005; Anthony and Govindarajan 2007).

The management accounting suggests different types of controls that can be implemented in organizations (Merchant 1998; Simons 2014; Drury 2016; Merchant and Van der Stede 2016):

- *Action or behavioural controls.* These controls are related to the definition, observation and monitoring of the behaviours of individuals during their work. They can take different forms: behavioural constraints, to prevent individuals from performing all or a portion of specific acts in the form of physical constraints (e.g. passwords) or administrative constraints (e.g. restriction of decision-making authority or separation of duties); pre-action reviews, to approve or disapprove the proposed plans, ask for modification, or require a more carefully considered plan before the final approval; action accountability, to make individuals aware of which actions are acceptable or unacceptable and make them accountable for the corresponding compliance with pre-specified work rules and procedures and codes of conduct.
- *Results or output controls.* These controls refer to the collection and reporting of information concerning the outcomes of the organizational

action. The implementation of results controls requires four steps: establishing those performance dimensions that are desirable, and defining the corresponding performance indicators; establishing performance targets; measuring the performance of the defined dimensions; defining rewards (or punishments) to motivate the behaviours that are expected to generate the desired results.

- *Personnel controls.* These controls concentrate on the tendencies of individuals to control themselves and do a good job, by making sure that they have a clear idea of what is expected from them and that they have the right capabilities and resources to perform their work. These controls leverage on a variety of elements such as intrinsic motivation, organizational atmosphere, loyalty and ethics, and morality. Personnel controls are implemented through selection and placement procedures, training programmes and job design, and provision of resources.
- *Clan and social controls.* Clan controls refer to the development of a community characterized by a strong sense of solidarity and commitment towards organizational goals, whereas social controls relate to a common understanding of what are accepted norms and patterns of behavior so that those that do not meet them are subject to some form of social punishment (e.g. signals of disapproval by the other organizational members and corresponding behaviours).

Some combination of all these controls is applied in any organization, but in an auditing environment, behaviour and output controls seem to have only limited effectiveness. Though it is possible to specify and monitor certain actions (e.g. timeliness), the key dimensions of behaviours (e.g. the level of performance in the different phases of the auditing process) cannot be directly observed. The quality of the auditing work is, in fact, the result of effective activities to be carried out, which cannot be easily assessed by means of measureable, delivered outputs. In addition, the comparison of the resources used in task performance against predefined budgets has only a restricted application, and needs to be combined with other quality assurance procedures. As a result, the key mechanisms to control the auditing setting are represented by personnel and clan/social controls. However, given that these are mainly qualitative, some tensions may emerge between the use of tight resources controls, such as time budgets, and the achievement of satisfactory quality targets. This is because the focus on more quantitative forms of control can generate some conflicts between resources and quality targets and lead to some undesired dysfunctional behaviours. This is particularly important in auditing firms because the quality is to a great extent the result of the judgement and integrity of auditors (Otley and Pierce 1996; Sweeney and Pierce 2004; Pierce and Sweeney 2005; Anthony and Govindarajan 2007).

Technocratic and socio-ideological forms of control in auditing firms

An alternative theoretical perspective with which to look at auditing firms is the institutional-constructivist view. According to this latter, auditing firms are knowledge-intensive firms that provide institutional myths because they are characterized by ambiguities and uncertainties in their activities and outputs. According to this logic, auditing firms have to stress, both internally and externally, in relation to the various stakeholders, that their experts should be relied upon. In addition, they have to develop an elaborated language code through which to describe themselves and their organization, and regulate client orientations as well as identity (Alvesson 1993). Furthermore, their knowledge plays roles such as (1) a mode of developing a community and social identity by means of providing individuals in the organization a shared language and promoting self-esteem, (2) a resource for persuading the public and the clients, (3) a means to develop a company's profile (an image to use in the market), (4) a channel to create legitimacy and trust concerning activities and results, and (5) a conduit for obscuring uncertainty and counteracting reflection. With these roles assigned to knowledge, the management of auditing firms would be more related to influencing employees, including securing and developing work and organizational identity (Alvesson 1993; Ditillo 2004). This latter points at an affiliation with the organization and charges the affiliation with emotional significance and personal meaning. Organizational identity has a critical role for the firm because it provides clues for action, interpretation and conduct. It is acquired by means of identification processes, which can be affected. In this respect, organizational identity drives organizational action and therefore can operate as a means of management control (Kärreman and Alvesson 2004).

With these premises, it is important to recognize that structural forms of control never exist in a culture-free context, but operate in the realm of a specific organizational identity. Focused on behaviour and/or measurable output, they are reinforced and complemented, sometimes perhaps challenged or contradicted by, cultural ideas and values. For this reason, it is important to analyze the interfaces between certain structural arrangements and the ideologies and norms targeting how individuals are supposed to think, feel and act. A critical aspect is related to how a high level of compliance – which incorporates willingness to work very long hours and pursue very difficult goals in terms of meeting deadlines and generating high margins in projects – is achieved. This requires the consideration of how the various forms of technocratic control interact and merge with socio-ideological modes of control (Alvesson and Kärreman 2004). Technocratic controls concentrate on the behavioural level, but they also produce a socio-ideological influence, as they are a means for creating and maintaining shared understanding and shared meanings. In fact, the same manuals, work methodologies, career steps, and hierarchies foster the development of a common identity (Kärreman and Alvesson 2004). The systems do not function entirely as a result of an effective technical design. They work in relationship to and contribute to the shaping of a specific "interpretive community" and assessment of the techniques. Technocratic controls work efficiently when their messages find a receptive audience gradually formed by the control, delivery and feedback cultures. At the same time, socio-ideological forms are important inputs to this gradually increasing receptivity. The symbolism and powers of these forms in shaping thinking, feeling and identifying are central in developing a technocratic culture. Seen in this way, technocratic and socio-ideological forms of control interact a may merge and, sometimes, contradict each other.

Knowledge-management strategies

In knowledge-intensive firms, performance highly depends on the expertise of individuals, which is exceptional and valuable and dominates common knowledge (Starbuck 1992; Ditillo 2004; Jääskeläinen and Laihonen 2013). This expertise involves the technical skills stressed in the formal qualifications of professionals, the interpersonal skills necessary to interact within and beyond the boundaries of the organization, and client knowledge, which is an important source of power and prestige (Morris and Empson 1998). Besides this expertise, knowledge is also incorporated in the firm's job descriptions, manuals and procedures, routines, software and professional cultures (Starbuck 1992; Kärreman & Alvesson 2004).

Because of the multifaceted nature of the expertise of knowledge-intensive firms, different types of interaction have to be activated in order to transfer and integrate knowledge (Marin, Cordier, and Hameed 2016): socialization, related to the process by which tacit knowledge possessed by one individual, or a restricted group of individuals, is transformed into tacit knowledge shared by a larger community; externalization, referring to the articulation of tacit knowledge into explicit knowledge by means of interaction and collective sense-making of individuals and groups; combination, linked to the merging of different sets of knowledge into more complex and articulated forms of explicit knowledge; and, finally, internalization, related to the conversion of explicit knowledge into tacit knowledge by means of direct experience and learning by doing (Nonaka and Takeuchi 1995).

Knowledge-intensive firms may adopt alternative strategies of knowledge management. One possibility is knowledge codification by means of which knowledge can be appropriated and replicated across the organization. An alternative strategy may be to collectivize knowledge without codifying a substantial amount of it. Knowledge-intensive firms need to decide how to position themselves in the level of codification and activate suitable corresponding organizational mechanisms for knowledge integration and transfer (Morris and Empson 1998; Kaše, Paauwe, and Zupan 2009; Marin, Cordier, and Hameed 2016).

References

Alvesson, M. (1993) Organizations as rhetoric: Knowledge-intensive firms and the struggle with ambiguity. *Journal of Management Studies, 30*(6), 997–1015.

Alvesson, M., and Kärreman, D. (2004) Interfaces of control: Technocratic and socio-ideological control in a global management consultancy firm. *Accounting, Organizations and Society, 29*(3), 423–444.

Anthony, R. N., and Govindarajan, V. (2007) *Management Control Systems*. Singapore: McGrawHill.

Barber, F., and Strack, R. (2005) The surprising economics of a "people business". *Harvard Business Review, 83*(6), 80–90.

Ditillo, A. (2004) Dealing with uncertainty in knowledge-intensive firms: The role of management control systems as knowledge integration mechanisms. *Accounting, Organizations and Society, 29*(3), 401–421.

Drury, C. (2016) *Management Accounting for Business*. 6th ed. London: Cengage Learning.

Ekstedt, E. (1989) Knowledge renewal and knowledge companies. *Research Report No. 22*, Uppsala Papers in Economic History, 1–17.

Greenwood, R., Hinings, C. R., and Brown, J. (1990) "P2-form" strategic management: Corporate practices in professional partnerships. *Academy of Management Journal, 33*(4), 725–755.

Hinings, C. R., Brown, J. L., and Greenwood, R. (1991) Change in an autonomous professional organization. *Journal of Management Studies, 28*(4), 375–393.

Jääskeläinen, A., and Laihonen, H. (2013) Overcoming the specific performance measurement challenges of knowledge-intensive organizations. *International Journal of Productivity and Performance Management, 62*(4), 350–363.

Kärreman, D., and Alvesson, M. (2004) Cages in tandem: Management control, social identity, and identification in a knowledge-intensive firm. *Organization, 11*(1), 149–175.

Kaše, R., Paauwe, J., and Zupan, N. (2009) HR practices, interpersonal relations, and intrafirm knowledge transfer in knowledge-intensive firms: A social network perspective. *Human Resource Management, 48*(4), 615–639.

Maister, D. H. (1982) Balancing the professional service firm. *Sloan Management Review, 24*(1), 15.

Maister, D. H. (1993) *Managing the Professional Firm*. New York: Free Press.

Marin, A., Cordier, J., and Hameed, T. (2016) Reconciling ambiguity with interaction: Implementing formal knowledge strategies in a knowledge-intensive organization. *Journal of Knowledge Management, 20*(5), 959–979.

Merchant, K. A. (1998) *Modern Management Control Systems*. Upper Saddle River: Prentice Hall.

Merchant, K. A., and Van der Stede, W. A. (2016) *Management Control Systems: Performance Measurement, Evaluation and Incentives*. 3rd ed. Harlow: Pearson Education.

Morris, T., and Empson, L. (1998) Organisation and expertise: An exploration of knowledge bases and the management of accounting and consulting firms. *Accounting, Organizations and Society, 23*(5), 609–624.

Nonaka, I., and Takeuchi, H. (1995) *The Knowledge-Creating Company: How Japanese Companies Create the Dynamics of Innovation*. Oxford: Oxford University Press.

Otley, D. T., and Pierce, B. J. (1996) The operation of control systems in large audit firms. *Auditing: A Journal of Practice and Theory, 15*(2), 65.

Pierce, B., and Sweeney, B. (2005) Management control in audit firms – Partners' perspectives. *Management Accounting Research, 16*(3), 340–370.

Schriesheim, J., Von Glinow, M. A., and Kerr, S. (1977) Professionals in bureaucracies: A structural alternative, in: Paul C. Nystrom and William H. Starbuck, eds., *Prescriptive Models of Organizations*, 55–69. Amsterdam: North-Holland Publishing Co.

Simons, R. (2014) *Performance Measurement and Control Systems for Implementing Strategy*. First New International Edition. Harlow: Pearson Education.

Starbuck, W. H. (1992) Learning by knowledge-intensive firms. *Journal of Management Studies, 29*(6), 713–740.

Sweeney, B., and Pierce, B. (2004) Management control in audit firms: A qualitative examination. *Accounting, Auditing & Accountability Journal, 17*(5), 779–812.

Von Nordenflycht, A. (2010) What is a professional service firm? Toward a theory and taxonomy of knowledge-intensive firms. *Academy of Management Review, 35*(1), 155–174.

Winch, G., and Schneider, E. (1993) Managing the knowledge-based organization: The case of architectural practice. *Journal of Management Studies, 30*(6), 923–937.

3 Individual auditors

Introduction

Regulators and professional bodies around the world are aware of the importance of auditors' individual characteristics and set different requirements that people should meet in order to become and remain (i.e. for their continuing professional development) certified auditors (e.g. Directive 2006/43/ EC of the European Parliament and of the Council[1] and IES 8 issued by IAESB[2]). All of the above is in the spirit of serving the public interest, by contributing to the ability of the auditing profession to meet the needs of the persons who rely on the opinion expressed in the audit reports. In addition, auditing firms consider people selection as one of their key processes because, as suggested by Milgrom and Roberts (1992), the most important specialized input in partnerships is typically their human capital (i.e. the knowledge and ability of workers).

Looking at the audit process, "audits are of higher quality [at the input level] when the people implementing audit tests are competent and independent [. . .] and make good decisions regarding the specific tests to be implemented and appropriately evaluate the evidence from these tests in leading to the audit report" (Francis 2011: 126).

In the academic literature, different approaches are used in order to determine which individual auditors' characteristics matter. Here a summary of the auditing research when dealing with the most studied individual auditor characteristics/attributes is presented. Notice that a comprehensive review is beyond the scope of this chapter and thus I focus on the most important/ studied individual factors, mainly looking at the articles published in top accounting and auditing journals. However, a rather detailed approach is used, with the purpose of introducing the relevant individual attributes as the basis for setting the ground to examine the auditors' behaviours within the teams, which is the object of the following chapters and the core of this book.

For reaching the chapter's purpose, auditing judgement and decision-making (JDM) research is relevant, as it aims at understanding individual and group judgements and decisions (Trotman, Tan, and Ang 2011). JDM research has a long tradition: it was the predominant paradigm in auditing in the 1970s and 1980s (Gibbins and Swieringa 1995). In a nutshell, the objective of these studies is to evaluate auditors' judgement quality, to describe how judgements are made, which factors impact on them and why (i.e. to understand auditors' cognitive processes that support auditors' judgements and decisions) and to develop tools to improve auditors' judgements. To reach the chapter's goal, I examine JDM research focusing on individual auditor's judgements, which constitutes the major part of it (Trotman, Bauer, and Humphreys 2015). It mainly relies on experimental method, referred as experimental psychology, even if some JDM studies build on economic theory in addition to the psychological one (for more details see Trotman et al. 2011: note 3).

Starting from the 1990s, archival studies became more and more widespread: among them there are studies, different from JDMs, that for example test the impact of individual auditor characteristics that could be inferred by public sources (like gender, age, type of education, etc.) on different observable audit outcomes. Quality of audited earnings, going concern audit reports, and audit fees paid for audit engagement are the most common empirical observables labelled as audit outcomes (Francis 2011; DeFond and Zhang 2014). Generally, these kinds of studies examine data concerning audit partner's characteristics. In fact, public data on signing partners (i.e. auditors who sign audit reports) are available in some research settings.[3] As signing partners plan and implement the audit and take the ultimate decision on the type of audit report to be issued to the client (Ferguson, Francis, and Stokes 2003), their characteristics should impact on the quality of the audit engagement (Chin and Chi 2009).

It is important to consider both experiments and archival research as their findings complement each other's. Differently from archival research, which can rely both on public or private data – the former represents by far the most common case[4] – experimental studies are based on an experimental design, allowing stronger casual inference (e.g. Libby and Luft 1993). Using experiments, individual auditor attributes like the level of professional scepticism and the cognitive and decision-making styles have been explored. Moreover, many experiments have been done involving not only partners, but also managers and juniors. This is relevant, as previous research has shown that judgement structures of more experienced auditors are substantially different from those of less experienced ones (e.g. Choo and Trotman 1991). On the contrary, archival research, due to data availability constraints, mainly focused on partners. However, many scholars have challenged and criticized the practical possibility to generalize experimental research, especially those performed in the laboratory (Dobbins, Lane, and Steiner 1988; Griffin and Kacmar 1991; Stone-Romero 2002; Greenberg and Tomlinson 2004), and those performed using exclusively students as subjects of the test (Gordon, Slade, and Schmitt 1986). The basic criticism is about the validity to replicate the experimental findings across different settings or populations (Campbell and Stanley 1963). Thus, in this chapter, I triangulate JDM findings with the ones of other types of empirical research, mainly the archival one. In addition, some relevant research using survey and field studies is included in the following pages (e.g. Kelley and Margheim 1990; Dalton, Buchheit, and McMillan 2014).

Furthermore, some studies that examine the impact of individual auditor's characteristics on audit processes/outcomes, using analytical models (e.g. Carcello and Santore 2015) are presented. These models employed mathematical representations, economic theory, and logic for the analysis of the selected phenomenon (Vasarhelyi 1982).

Are auditors' judgements and audit outcomes the same for any individual auditor?

From a theoretical point of view, before examining what are the individual auditor's characteristics that influence an auditor's judgement and audit outcomes, it should be questioned whether the so-called individual auditor effect exists: i.e. do auditors' judgements and audit outcomes vary for different individual auditors?

Building on behavioural decision theory, ability, knowledge, motivation, and environment are examined as determinants of decision performance in accounting settings (Bonner and Lewis 1990; Libby and Luft 1993; Libby 1995). Indeed, innate ability influences knowledge acquisition and thus task performance. To explore this, JDM researchers generally use experiments, as knowledge is not directly observable (Libby and Luft 1993). They construct experimental tasks where knowledge differentiation is predicted because of differences between individuals. Then, they measure performance variation among the participants (Bedard and Biggs 1991; Libby and Luft 1993). These variations were documented in many of these studies; for a review please refer to Trotman et al. (2011) and to Nelson and Tan (2005).

Looking outside this stream of research, there is an increasing interest in considering the individual auditor as the unit of analysis. DeFond and Francis (2005) argue that the determinants of audit quality could be found at individual partner level. More recently, doing a review of archival non-JDM auditing research, DeFond and Zhang (2014) call upon researchers to investigate the association between individual auditor characteristics and audit quality.

Focusing on non-JDM archival research, Knechel, Vanstraelen, and Zerni (2015), mainly using Swedish data on private companies, suggest that aggressive or conservative audit reporting is a systematic partner attribute. Li, Qi, Tian, and Zhang (2016) examine the relation between individual auditors' audit failures (i.e. auditors whose client/s subsequently restated reported earnings downwards) and the quality of other audits conducted by the same auditors. The setting used is the Chinese one. They document that these auditors also deliver lower quality audits on other audit engagements. Wang, Yu, and Zhao (2015), using the same setting, examine the relation between partner failure rate (i.e. the total number of audit failures – measured by restatements – associated with an audit partner divided by the total number of audit reports signed by the same partner) and audit quality. They document that an audit partner's past audit failure rate is positively associated with the probability that her clients' current year annual report is subsequently restated.

Looking at the capital market in Taiwan, Aobdia, Lin, and Petacchi (2015) show that this market recognizes and values higher quality audit partners (proxied by accrual quality of the partner's clients). They find a positive association between earnings response coefficients and individual partners' quality, suggesting that investors perceive earnings to be more informative when higher quality partners perform the audit. They also find that the markets react positively when the client firm switches from a lower quality partner to a higher quality partner: their results show that firms audited by higher quality partners experience a lower level of underpricing when they go public. This positive effect is documented not only for the equity markets, but also for the debt markets. Indeed, Aobdia et al. (2015) find that firms audited by higher quality partners pay lower interest rates, have greater access to credit, and are less likely to be required to post collaterals.

Chen, Peng, Xue, Yang, and Ye (2016) conclude the introduction of their study in the Chinese setting arguing that the empirical evidence that auditees successfully engage in partner-level opinion shopping constitutes a new, robust evidence that individual auditors – even those affiliated with the same audit firm – exhibit significant variation in audit quality. Taylor (2011) documents that different audit partners – even from the same audit firm – can earn significantly different levels of audit fee premiums, suggesting that this is due to partners' capabilities of providing different audit process quality levels.

Gul, Wu, and Yang (2013) show that signing auditors affect audit quality in China and this can be partly due to their individual characteristics. They document that partner effect is relevant after controlling for client characteristics and the concurrent effects of audit firms and audit offices.[5] Indeed, audit firms and engagement offices' procedures would standardize the behavior of partners within the firm and within specific engagement offices.[6]

Hsieh and Lin (2016), examining listed firms in Taiwan, question whether an auditor's industry expertise affects firms' client acceptance decisions, distinguishing between partner-level and firm-level industry specialization. Findings show that industry expertise is not homogeneous across individuals, having partners a clear incentive to protect their reputations when making client acceptance decisions, as their identity is publicly disclosed in Taiwan. To give a complete picture, also studies questioning whether the engagement partner signature is associated with audit judgements and outcomes should be examined.

The request of personal sign off has been considered as an accountability mechanism (PCAOB 2015). Individual auditor performance is subject to both internal (e.g. inside the audit firms) and external (e.g. by regulators) monitoring. Behavioral research documents a positive relation between accountability and auditor effort (e.g. Asare, Trompeter, and Wright 2000; DeZoort, Harrison, and Taylor 2006). Moreover, when auditors' identity becomes observable by a much larger audience, according to previous JDM research findings, this would provide additional motivation for auditors to do a better job. For example Messier, Quilliam, Hirst, and Craig (1992) document that greater accountability is related to an increase in cognitive processing by auditors. Hoffman and Patton (1997) find that accountability led to more conservative fraud risk judgements. More generally, accountability reduces decision biases (Kennedy 1993; Brazel, Agoglia, and Hatfield 2004).

Using an analytical model, Carcello and Santore (2015) show a positive relation between partner signature requirement and auditor decision to collect more evidence. Carcello and Li (2013) archival findings concerning UK listed companies are consistent with the argument of improved audit outcomes after the adoption of partner signature requirement. Investigating the effect of the engagement partner signature requirement on financial markets (once again in the United Kingdom), Liu (2016) shows that the adoption of the signature requirement improves analysts' information environment. This is partially due to higher audit quality.

All above documents that, according to previous literature, there are differences in individual auditors' judgements and outcomes.

Individual auditor characteristics affecting auditors' judgements and audit outcomes

In this section, I present the most studied auditor characteristics for which previous studies documented a significant impact on auditors' judgements and audit outcomes. Nelson and Tan (2005: 41) classify JDM literature as covering three broad areas: i.e. the audit task, the auditor and her attributes, and interaction between auditor and other stakeholders in task performance. Given the aim of this chapter, the second area is the one of main interest here. As explained in the introduction (to this chapter), considering both experiments and archival research is important, as their findings complement each other's. Thus, I also draw on non-JDM archival evidence to triangulate JDM research findings. As an example, Gul et al. (2013) explore a number of auditor characteristics to better understand the factors which may drive systematic partner style effects, suggesting that educational background, Big N audit firm experience, rank in the audit firm, and political affiliation are important. Other non-JDM empirical studies show that individual partner's characteristics such as gender, age, experience, industry expertise, and partner tenure with the client may also be associated with audit outcomes (e.g. Carey and Simnett 2006; Chin and Chi 2009; Zerni 2012; Goodwin and Wu 2014; Sundgren and Svanstrom 2014; Hardies, Breesch, and Branson 2015; Wang et al. 2015). Consequently, having Nelson and Tan (2005) classification in mind,[7] I grouped the auditing studies on individual auditor attributes in research related to personal traits (demographic traits and other traits) and to auditor knowledge (education, general audit experience, and auditor expertise). Moreover, I offer a brief summary of the most studied individual interactional variables on the impact of personal traits and knowledge on an auditor's performance, such as her busyness, tenure, social ties, and mood and emotional states. Figure 3.1 illustrates the framework used for summarizing previous literature on an individual auditor's characteristics.

Personal traits

The word "traits" indicates dispositional differences to think, feel, and behave in a consistent way that can be activated by environmental pressures and life events (Schmitt, Realo, Voracek, and Allik 2008). The underlying assumption is that traits are stable over time and that they influence individuals' behaviours. Although there is probably a circular effect as traits influence behaviours and behaviours affect the traits, the general assumption is that dominant direction of causality is from traits to behaviours (Matthews, Deary, and Whiteman 2003). Thus, personal traits capture consistent behaviour responses of an individual when facing similar situations across time (Bem and Allen 1974). Of course, having similar traits does not imply that the individuals will certainly behave in the same way across a variety of situations, but that they have a higher propensity to a certain reaction. In the previous audit literature, auditor's behaviours are related to different clusters of traits. In the following pages the most examined are presented, grouped in the ones related to demographic characteristics (gender, age and national

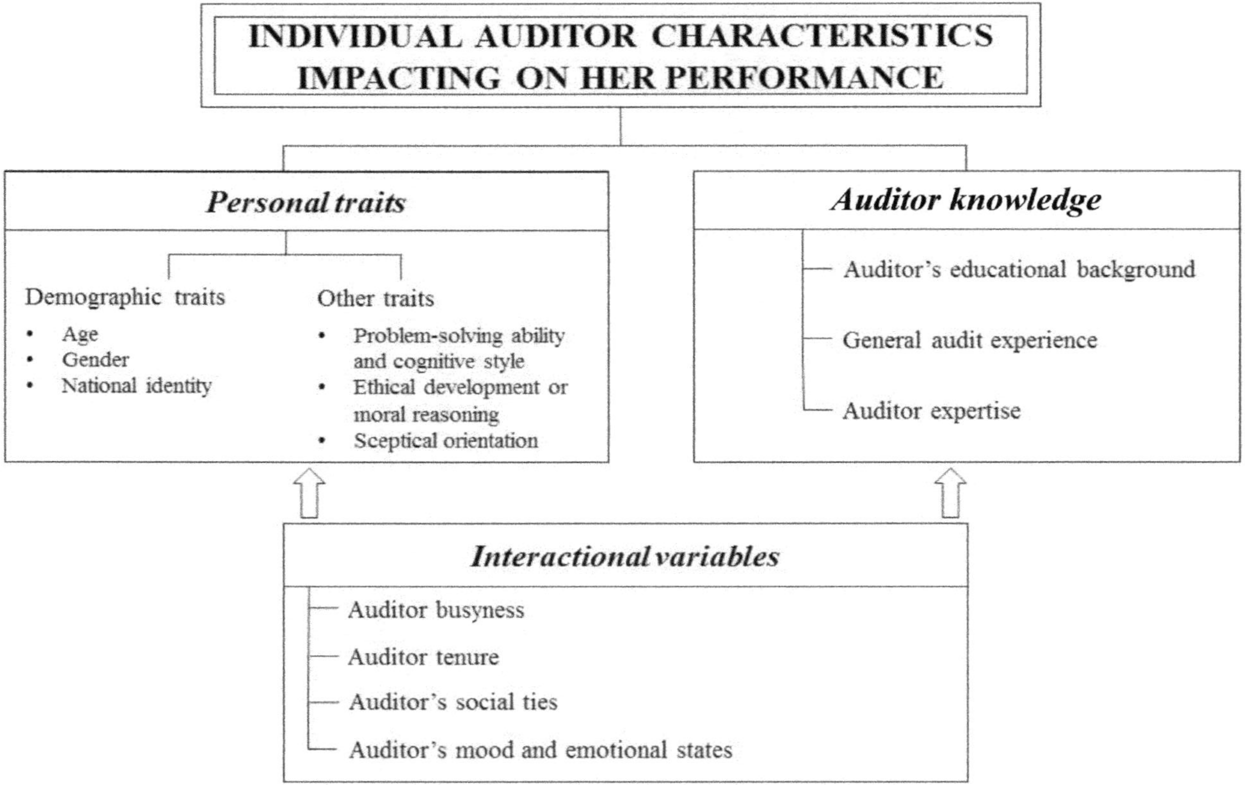

INDIVIDUAL AUDITOR CHARACTERISTICS IMPACTING ON HER PERFORMANCE

Personal traits

Demographic traits
- Age
- Gender
- National identity

Other traits
- Problem-solving ability and cognitive style
- Ethical development or moral reasoning
- Sceptical orientation

Auditor knowledge
- Auditor's educational background
- General audit experience
- Auditor expertise

Interactional variables
- Auditor busyness
- Auditor tenure
- Auditor's social ties
- Auditor's mood and emotional states

Figure 3.1 Individual auditor characteristics

identities) and the other traits such as problem-solving ability and cognitive style, ethical development or moral reasoning, and sceptical orientation.

Demographic traits

Under this label, I present the results of the studies that consider auditor's age, gender, and national identities. As better explained later in the section, some of these are also used as proxies of other auditor's attributes that do not fall into the demographic label (e.g. age as a proxy of auditor's general professional experience).

Psychology, behavioural economics as well as the audit literature (e.g. Chung and Monroe 2001) show that *gender*-based differences can affect the quality of the work done by the individuals. Literature in the fields of psychology and behavioural economics documents gender-based differences in cognitive information processing, conservatism, diligence, and risk tolerance (e.g. Byrnes, Miller, and Schafer 1999; Schmitt et al. 2008; Croson and Gneezy 2009). Also, the audit literature explores gender issues, traditionally using experiments (e.g. Chung and Monroe 2001; O'Donnell and Johnson 2001). Overall, the results maintain that an auditor's gender affects audit judgement. In particular, these studies document that female auditors are more accurate and effective in information processing. Female auditors also show lower intentions to engage in audit quality reduction behaviours (Sweeney, Arnold, and Pierce 2010), are less concerned with the commercial side of auditing (Jonnergård, Stafsudd, and Elg 2010), and are generally more ethical (e.g. Bernardi and Arnold 1997). In addition, some non-JDM archival studies deal with this issue. Based on a sample of Finnish and Swedish listed companies, Ittonen, Vähämaa, and Vähämaa (2013) document that female partners are associated with higher accrual quality. Using going concern opinions (GCOs) as an indicator of audit quality, Hardies, Breesch, and Branson (2016) document for a sample of private Belgian companies that female auditors are more likely to issue GCOs than male auditors. Thus, the authors (Hardies et al. 2016) conclude that their findings indicate higher audit quality by female auditors.[8] However, using a large sample of Chinese data, Gul et al. (2013) do not find that a partner's gender matters in explaining audit quality. Using the same setting, Li et al. (2016) reported that "negative" contagion effect of auditors who have experienced audit failures in the past is moderated by gender, being female auditors associated to higher audit quality audits.

Studies by Ittonen and Peni (2012) and Hardies et al. (2015) find that audit fees are different in relation to an auditor's gender.

A second demographic variable considered by previous literature is *age*. Behavioral economics and psychology research suggest that effort and experience are functions of age (e.g. Bonner and Lewis 1990; Holmström 1999; Morris and Venkatesh 2000). For example in the last stage of a worker carrier, she prepares for the forthcoming retirement by disengaging from the job, which results in lower performance. It could also be that older auditors are more indulgent with their clients. As audit quality is shaped by the incentives of individual auditors, in the last phase of an auditor's carrier concerns regarding reputation maintenance are less relevant. Sundgren and Svanstrom (2014) document that older auditors (partners) are less likely to issue a going-concern opinion (associated with lower audit quality). Their findings are consistent with Goodwin and Wu (2016), who show that partner's age is generally negatively associated with audit quality.

Goodwin and Wu (2016) and Sundgren and Svanstrom (2014) underline that age can also be used as a proxy of general auditor experience. In fact, both "experience is functions of age" (Sundgren and Svanstrom 2014: 531) and "the experience variable is strongly correlated with partner age" (Goodwin and Wu 2016: footnote 13). Following, in the part related to auditor knowledge, the findings of previous studies focusing on the impact on auditor's judgements and outcomes of her general audit experience are reported.

Regarding *national identities*, numerous JDM researchers (e.g. Hong, Morris, Chiu, and Benet-Martinez 2000; Morris and Fu 2001; Wong and Hong 2005; Weber and Morris 2010) show that differences in individuals' judgements and decisions depend on cultural values and beliefs. This is in line with the management literature that shows that culture acquired in childhood (Hofstede 1983) and cultural and educational-based factors (e.g. House, Hanges, Javidan, Dorfman, and Gupta 2004) affect management decisions.

In a quite recent synthesis, Nolder and Riley (2014) identified five categories of auditors' judgements and decisions (namely, auditors' confidence, risk and probability judgements, risk decisions, conflict decisions, and ethical judgements) that are most likely to be affected by cross-cultural differences, generally measured by auditor's nationality. For example there is some evidence that Asians (with the exception of Japanese) are more overconfident than Americans or Europeans (e.g. Wright and Phillips 1980; Yates, Lee, Shinotsuka, Patalano, and Sieck 1998). This might affect auditors' judgement and decisions (Nolder and Riley 2014). Some researchers (e.g. O'Donnell and Prather-Kinsey 2010) document significant cross-cultural differences in risk or probability judgement, while others (e.g. Yamamura, Frakes, Sanders, and Ahn 1996) find no differences. At the same time, there is supporting evidence on significant associations between culture and auditor risk decisions. For example Arnold, Bernardi, and Neidermeyer (2001) show that US auditors are more risk adverse in assessing materiality levels than auditors in Denmark, Ireland, Italy, Spain,

Sweden, the United Kingdom, and The Netherlands. Thereafter, concerning conflict decisions, the premise is that some cultures are more likely to "go along to get along" than others (Nolder and Riley 2014) and this may affect conflict decisions involving an auditor and a client or an auditor and a superior. For example Lin and Fraser (2008) document that "collectivist" Chinese auditors are more likely to align to client preferences than individualist UK auditors. Finally, culture was associated with variations in auditors' ethical judgements. As an example, Cohen, Pant, and Sharp (1995) study the ethical judgements of 138 auditors from the United States, Japan, and Latin America, using eight cases depicted in vignettes. Overall, the strongest differences were found between Latin American auditors (belonging to a culture considered as a high collectivist and high power distance) and US auditors (highly individualist and low power distance culture). Latin American auditors in comparison to the US ones perceived the actions described in the vignettes as significantly less ethical.

Other traits

Clearly, any auditor has an enormous number of traits, different from the ones reported under the label of demographic traits, which could potentially influence her decisions, but audit literature until now has focused on three: problem-solving ability and cognitive style, individual ethical development or moral reasoning, and sceptical orientation. Recall that the word "traits" is used to indicate dispositional differences to think, feel, and behave in a consistent way that can be activated by environmental pressures and life events (Schmitt et al. 2008). In the previous research, the impact of other traits has been studied. For example Amir, Kallunki, and Nilsson (2014) use a proprietary data set from Sweden to examine whether audit partners' personal risk preferences affect client portfolio decisions. In particular, criminal convictions are used as a proxy for audit partners' personal risk preference (i.e. a proxy for audit partners' propensity to take audit risks). Results show that audit partners with criminal convictions engage in riskier audits and that their clients report less conservatively. Cohen and Trompeter (1998) in large accounting firms find that the more aggressive the partners, the more likely they are to accept the client's relatively aggressive accounting choices.

The widely used Libby and Luft model (Libby and Luft 1993) predicts performance as function of ability, knowledge, environment, and motivation. The traditional way to measure ability in the audit field is through auditor's *problem-solving ability*. Problem-solving ability is the ability to underscore relations, interpret data, and reason analytically (Bonner and Lewis 1990). It is partially innate but it could be refined through experience. The problem-solving ability of a person has been sometimes equated to her intellectual skills (e.g. Palmer, Ziegenfuss, and Pinsker 2004).

Overall, previous research, using different measure to assess problem-solving ability of the auditors (e.g. Bonner and Lewis 1990; Bonner and Walker 1994; Libby and Tan 1994; Bierstaker and Wright 2001) has documented that the higher the problem-solving ability, the higher her performance.

Other studies operationalize the ability in the abovementioned Libby and Luft model as *cognitive style* (e.g. Fuller and Kaplan 2004; Bryant, Murthy, and Wheeler 2009). Cognitive style represents the preferred method of acquiring and processing information during a problem-solving process (Ho and Rodger 1993). Building on personality type theory (Jung 1921; Myers, McCaulley, Quenk, and Hammer 1998) that defines personality using four dimensions (i.e. extroversion–introversion, sensor–intuitive, thinking–feeling, and judging–perceiving), the sensor–intuitive and thinking–feeling dimensions have been used to measure cognitive style in accounting literature (Bryant et al. 2009), as one trait in each pair is dominant (Wheeler, Hunton, and Bryant 2004). For example in a bankruptcy prediction task, Casey (1980) documented that intuitives outperformed sensors in overall accuracy, whereas Rodgers and Housel (1987) found that sensors performed better than intuitives in a bank loan decision task. Fuller and Kaplan (2004) findings show that a misfit between the task attributes (detailed-oriented vs pattern-oriented) and the auditor's cognitive style could explain these mixed results. Indeed, their results show that sensor auditors performed better on workpaper review task (i.e. detailed-oriented), while intuitive auditors performed better on the analytical review task (i.e. pattern-oriented task). Thus, there is empirical support for cognitive style affecting performance in the auditing setting. Of course, the moderating effect of other factors should be considered, such as the abovementioned task attributes as well as the effects of providing different types of feedback on the individual performance (Bryant et al. 2009).

There is a wide consensus between practitioners and scholars in considering ethical conduct as the cornerstone of the auditing profession. Thus, exploring the factors influencing it is of utmost importance. Kohlberg's (1969) theory of cognitive development is the framework used in the majority of studies on auditors' ethical reasoning (Jones, Massey, and Thorne 2003). Drawing upon this theory, "Rest (1979, 1994) identified four sequential components of the ethical reasoning process: sensitivity in identifying the existence of a moral question, ethical evaluation, intention to act morally and actual moral behavior" (Sweeney et al. 2010: 532). The main idea is that individual *ethical development or moral reasoning* depends on the individual moral consciousness and it influences the way a person deals with conflicts or dilemmas in everyday practice. Applied to the audit environment, it reflects the auditor's ability to neutralize her judgement from self-interest and to identify the relevance of her actions on the decisions of other people (Ponemon and Gabhart 1994; Jones et al. 2003). The results of studies analyzing this dimension are quite consistent with the idea that auditors with higher moral attitudes are less likely to accept aggressive reporting and are better able to identify potential inappropriate behaviors (e.g. Bernardi 1994; Schatzberg, Sevcik, Shapiro, Thorne, and Wallace 2005). In addition, previous research (e.g. Bernardi and Arnold 2004) prove that the auditor's moral level is positively associated with the experience and that audit firms tend to retain the auditors with higher moral reasoning levels. In this sense, the auditor's ethical reasoning is analyzed also as a consequence of and in relation to her experience. Moreover, as illustrated in the section devoted to demographic traits, there is an empirical documented relation between cultural beliefs and moral reasoning, as earlier studies had reported ethical differences among auditors raised in different countries (e.g. Patel, Harrison, and McKinnon 2002; Spicer, Dunfee, and Bailey 2004; Arnold, Bernardi, Neidermeyer, and Schmee 2007; Bailey and Spicer 2007).

Finally, professional scepticism is one of the main pillars of the auditing profession. It has been defined by many different sources, including different accounting bodies and standard setters, and the common elements of these definitions are the focus on the processes of gathering and analyzing evidence, its critical assessment, and the need to maintain a questioning mind (Nelson 2009). From a theoretical point of view, having a more *sceptical orientation* affects auditors' performances in a positive way as it implies more sceptical judgements and decisions, such as engaging in more substantive testing (Quadackers, Groot, and Wright 2014). It can be partially considered an innate trait of the individual (Hurtt 2010). When accounting researchers have decided to measure professional scepticism, they have both used scales designed to measure other constructs like trust (e.g. Shaub and Lawrence 1996; Choo and Tan 2000) or independence (Shaub 1996) and have also developed measures specific to their experimental condition (e.g. McMillan and White 1993), thus obtaining results that are difficult to compare. More recently, Hurtt (2010) has built an ex ante measure of an individual's level of trait of professional scepticism, assuming a neutral perspective (i.e. the auditor expects no bias in management's representations, ex ante). Quadackers et al. (2014) highlight that different measures of scepticism may be suitable for different audit settings in order to predict real auditors' judgements, thus using scales based on trust may be appropriate when professional scepticism is intended assuming a presumptive doubt perspective: that is, expecting some level of dishonesty or bias by auditee management's representations.

Overall, previous literature shows a positive relation between professional scepticism and audit quality (for a summary please refer to Knechel, Krishnan, Pevzner, Shefchik, and Velury 2013). Auditor's behaviour consistent with higher levels of professional scepticism has been also associated (positively) with individual ethical development and moral reasoning (e.g. Bernardi 1994; Brown-Liburd, Cohen, and Trompeter 2013).

Auditor knowledge

A large part of the JDM audit research has examined the relation between auditor knowledge and performance. Libby (1995) suggests that acquisition of knowledge is determined by instruction, experience, and ability. "Instruction may be received both formally and informally in college and through firm continuing education courses [. . .]. Individuals also might learn from practice in performing tasks and receiving feedback on their judgments" (Bonner and Walker 1994: 158). The classroom knowledge is the starting point, as both regulators (e.g. the Directive 2006/43/EC of the European Parliament and of the Council, mentioned in the introduction to this chapter) and standard setters around the world (e.g. IES 1[9] and IES 8[10] issued by IAESB) included some educational requirements in the prerequisites for entering into the profession.[11] Of course, auditor knowledge is also developed during professional activity. As Waller and Felix (1984: 383) point out, "the professional auditor acquires a complex network of knowledge over his or her years of experience: knowledge that simply cannot be obtained in the classroom." A summary of the most important studies exploring auditor knowledge follows, distinguishing among the ones related to an auditor's education background, general audit experience, and auditor expertise. The two latter being different, as expertise was defined as task/industry specific superior performance.

Auditor's educational background

Some studies have examined the impact of an auditor's educational background on audit performances. Results are mixed.

Very few studies focus on the effects of education on auditor's judgements. Among these, for example, Estes and Reames (1988) find no difference in auditors' material decisions based on various measures of education. Looking at the most recent non-JDM archival ones, Li et al. (2016) reported that "negative" contagion effect of auditors who have experienced audit failures is attenuated for auditors holding a master's degree (and auditors with more auditing experience). Also Gul et al. (2013), exploring a number of auditors' characteristics to better understand the factors that may drive systematic partner style effects, document that educational background matters. However, Cahan and Sun (2014) find no significant association between the signing partners' education level and neither of the audit outcomes' proxies used in their study.

General audit experience

A large body of research shows that audit performance increases in auditor experience (e.g. Libby and Frederick 1990; Simnett 1996; Lim and Tan 2010).

Frederick, Heiman-Hoffman, and Libby (1994) examine how the knowledge bases of the auditors differ according to individual levels of experience. They conducted an experiment involving audit managers, staff auditors (i.e. juniors), and students. Results show that audit knowledge is mostly gained from experience. A Libby and Luft (1993) study found that more experienced auditors do not always outperform less experienced ones. Anderson and Maletta (1994) document that experience is crucial when there is negative audit evidence, otherwise (i.e. when audit evidence is positive) the levels of experience have no impact. Shelton (1999) findings support the idea that experience reduces the influence of irrelevant information. Li et al. (2016), conducting an archival study, reported that "negative" contagion effect of auditors who have previously experienced audit failures is attenuated for auditors with more audit experience.

The impact of an auditor's general experience on her performance may depend on task complexity. Abdolmohammadi and Wright (1987) show that experienced auditors are able to make more accurate decisions about complex tasks than inexperienced auditors. More recently, Lehmann and Norman (2006) argue that more experienced individuals can solve complex problems better than less experienced ones due to their better knowledge structures. Using a sample of tax audits performed by the Croatian Tax Administration, Alissa, Capkun, Jeanjean, and Suca (2014) show, consistently with past experimental evidence, that auditor experience increases, while task complexity decreases, audit performance.

Auditor expertise

Bonner and Lewis (1990) document that general auditor experience is different from expertise, stating that a general experience variable is not a good proxy for expertise. Indeed, individuals with the same general experience may have, and generally have, different specific expertise.

Bedard and Biggs (1991), using an experiment based on a complex task which could be solved only by experienced auditors, find that it is the domain-specific experience (experience in the particular domain of the financial statement error) that improves professional judgement, not the general experience (i.e. number of years of experience). Many other experiments document that task-based experience enhances an auditor's performance (e.g. Libby and Tan 1994; Tan and Kao 1999; Thibodeau 2003). Indeed, task-based experience improves the quality of individual judgement by providing, for example, the opportunity to gain declarative knowledge (Bonner 1990; Choo and Trotman 1991; Bedard, Chi, Graham, and Shanteau 1993), error frequency knowledge (Ashton 1991), and meta-knowledge (Bédard et al. 1993).

In addition, among others, Hammersley (2006), Low (2004), Owhoso, Messier, and Lynch (2002) and Solomon, Shields, and Whittington (1999) have supported the idea that performance of industry-specialist auditors is superior in comparison to non-specialist auditors. Industry knowledge impacts on the auditor's judgement; for example industry specialists show more accurate non-error frequency knowledge (Solomon et al. 1999), more effective detection of errors during the review process (Owhoso et al. 2002) and more accurate assessment of audit risk (Low 2004). More recently, Moroney and Carey (2011) investigated the relative influence of industry and task-based experience on auditors, once again using an experiment. Results indicate that industry-based experience has a more significant impact on an auditor's performance than task-based experience. Tan and Libby (1997) and Kennedy and Peecher (1997) document for auditors the importance of tacit managerial knowledge (i.e. job knowledge on how to manage self, others, and career in a job setting).

Chin and Chi (2009) and Chi and Chin (2011) study the impact of audit partner's industry expertise on audit quality conducting a non-JDM archival research. Focusing on specialization in different industries in Taiwan, both studies document that audit partner's industry specialization is positively associated with audit quality. Ittonen, Johnstone, and Myllymäki (2015) show an association between audit partners' public-client specialization and audit quality proxied by abnormal accruals in Finland. In additional analyses, they also show that the public-client specialization appears to be most important for less experienced partners and that the association between public-client specialization and abnormal accruals is not linear. Indeed, they document that the negative relation between public-client specialization and abnormal accruals (i.e. less accrual, more audit quality) only occurs for partners with three to six public clients. For partners with seven or more public clients the "excessive" busyness seems to mitigate the benefits associated with this type of specialization. Zerni (2012) examines the relation between audit partner specialization and audit fees, looking also at specialization in public companies, using a sample of Swedish firms. Zerni's (2012) findings show that both industry specialization and specialization in public companies are associated with significant differences in the audit fees paid.

Individual interactional variables

Here are presented the most studied individual interactional variables associated with an auditor's performance in relation to the impact of personal traits and auditor knowledge on the former. I focus on the interactional variables related to individual auditors, starting from the most studied and then moving to the ones for which empirical support is more scant.

Auditor busyness

Auditors endure considerable stress, especially during busy season: they typically have multiple client engagements with multiple deadlines. If from one side this could make for incoming professionals the auditing relatively unattractive from a work-life balance perspective, inducing them to select alternative career paths, thus influencing the type of talent attracted to the profession (Dalton, Buchheit, and McMillan 2014), on the other side, it implies for actual auditors to cope with role stress. This may affect job outcomes.

Previous research found that for accounting professionals role stress has a negative impact on job outcomes (Jones, Norman, and Wier 2010). For example Sweeney and Summers (2002) show that busy season pressures are positively associated with public accountants' burnout. Cordes and Dougherty (1993) document that stress and burnout reduce individual performance, organizational attachment, and job satisfaction. McDaniel (1990) finds that audit effectiveness decreases with greater time pressure and Coram, Ng, and Woodliff (2004) show that auditors may undertake quality reduction acts as a strategic response to time pressures. Many other experimental and survey research indicates a reduction of an auditor's individual performance due to auditor burnout and time constraints (e.g. Kelley and Margheim 1990; McDaniel 1990; Raghunathan 1991; Willet and Page 1996; Cianci and Bierstaker 2009) and that time pressure leads to dysfunctional auditor behavior (e.g. McDaniel 1990; Malone and Roberts 1996; Otley and Pierce 1996; Willett and Page 1996).

Focusing on archival research, Sundgren and Svanstrom (2014) document a negative association between audit partner busyness (APB) – measured by the number of clients in an audit partner's portfolio in a year – and the propensity to issue a going-concern opinion (i.e. higher audit quality) before bankruptcy, for small and medium-sized Swedish clients. Karjalainen (2011) reports evidence of a positive relation between discretionary accruals (absolute value: the higher the accruals are the lower the audit quality) and APB, in the case of Big 4 auditors and large auditees, for private Finnish clients. However, more recently, Goodwin and Wu (2016), on the basis of the analysis of listed Australian companies, conclude that APB does not impair audit quality.

Cahan, Jeter, and Naiker (2011) provide archival evidence that APB is the result of strategic choices made by partners based on the comparative advantages in having multiple clients or focusing on a small number of clients.

Auditor tenure

As audit engagements are repeating,[12] some members of the previous year's audit team are generally reassigned to the same client. If, from one side, this increases an auditor's client-specific knowledge, then, on the other side, this may impair auditor independence and finally the auditor's performance.[13] The former may be due to the development of personal relationships between an auditor and her client, and/or to the deterioration in the auditor's capacity to effect critical appraisal, indicated as familiarity threat (Carey and Simnett 2006). Bamber and Iyer (2007) use Social Identity Theory (SIT) for explaining the potential negative effect on auditor independence of a close auditor-client relationship. SIT postulates that individuals who more strongly identify with a particular group are for example more likely to suppress their critical thinking or give the group an undue benefit (Ashforth and Mael 1989; Ashforth, Harrison, and Corley 2008). Sending a research questionnaire to a random sample of CPAs employed as auditors at Big 5 firms, Bamber and Iyer (2007) document that auditors with a stronger "client identity" are more likely to agree with a client-preferred accounting treatment. They also find that client identity strength is positively associated to auditor tenure, client image, and client importance. However, Bauer (2015), using an experimental setting with no prior auditor-client history, documents that even when auditor tenure is short, auditors may develop strong client identities and, as a consequence, their independence, objectivity, and professional scepticism might be undermined also in the absence of repeated auditor-client interactions, leading to relaxed agreements on the client's accounting preferences.

Archival research conducted in Australia (Ye, Carson, and Simnett 2011; Azizkhani, Monroe, and Shailer 2013) and China (Firth, Rui, and Wu 2012) shows a reduction in audit quality associated with long audit–partner tenure, whereas other research conducted in the United States (Manry, Mock, and Turner 2008) and Taiwan (Chen, Lin, and Lin 2008) does not find results consistent with this association. Bedard and Johnstone (2010) investigate the relation between audit partner tenure and audit planning and pricing. Using US proprietary data, they find a positive relation between audit partner tenure and planned realization rates, suggesting that engagements with longer partner tenure enable a greater return for the audit company. The study also reveals that there is no systematic difference in the planned effort for clients having long-tenure partners when compared to the effort for clients with short-tenure partners and that, consequently, the former engagements are not associated with lower quality (Bedard and Johnstone 2010). The relation between audit quality and partner tenure was studied also looking at mandatory partner rotation (i.e. imposed limit on the length of audit partner tenure). A forced change of audit partner may destroy/decrease an auditor's client-specific knowledge, but may improve audit quality by bringing a fresh perspective. Moreover, that change can provide a "peer review effect" of the incoming partner. For example Lennox, Wu, and Zhang (2014) test the impact of this rule on audit quality using a Chinese data set. Results document that forced rotation of engagement partners results in higher audit quality in the years immediately surrounding rotation (i.e. departing partner's final year and during the incoming partner's first year of tenure following mandatory rotation). However, Chi, Huang, Liao, and Xie (2009) archival study find little evidence that audit outcomes are affected by mandatory partner rotation. Stewart, Kent, and Routledge (2016) examine the relation between audit partner rotation and audit fees, using an Australian data set. They find a significant positive association between audit fees and both mandatory and voluntary partner rotation. However, additional analyses show differentiated findings across different segments of the audit market.

Auditor's social ties

In order to guarantee the independence of the public accounting profession and with specific reference to the auditing context, regulators around the world have stated rules that, for example, forbid auditees to engage, as principal auditor family members of their executives (e.g. SEC S7–13–00[14]; Directive 2006/43/Ec of the European Parliament and of the Council,[15] mentioned in the introduction to this chapter). However, auditors could have intense emotional attachments to persons different from their family members as well as be part of a network through which social ties are formed. The strength of connectedness within these networks can influence individual performances (Bruynseels and Cardinaels 2013).

Previous literature has explored how social ties impact on business decisions (e.g. Cohen, Frazzini, and Malloy 2010; Fracassi and Tate 2012; Nguyen 2012). With specific reference to auditors, some studies have examined settings where client companies hire former partners (e.g. Menon and Williams 2004; Lennox and Park 2007; Geiger, Lennox, and North 2008; Baber, Krishnan, and Zhang 2014). Overall results show impaired audit quality: both examining the impact on earnings quality (e.g. Menon and Williams 2004) and on investor perceptions (e.g. Baber et al. 2014). Regarding the former type of studies, results might be explained by the impact of cozy relation between former audit team members on auditor independence of continuing auditors, as well as by the superior knowledge and ability of affiliated executives with prior experience at the audit firm to circumvent effective audit procedures (Lennox 2005). Evidence on capital market (Baber et al. 2014) suggests that investors perceive that such hires impair audit quality even when according to earnings quality measures there is no difference (i.e. no impact on the quality of earnings reported by companies hiring former partners), thus affecting the perceived auditor independence.[16]

More recently Guan, Su, Wu, and Yang (2015), using a Chinese setting, identify auditors who attended the same university as the executives of their clients. Overall, findings show lower audit quality when auditors and client executives have school ties. This kind of result may be explained using for example arguments from the social identity theory (SIT), briefly illustrated in the previous auditor tenure section.

Auditor's mood and emotional states

Both psychology (e.g. Finucane, Alhakami, Slovic, and Johnson 2000; Peters, Västfjäll, Gärling, and Slovic 2006) and accounting literature (e.g. Kida and Smith 1995; Moreno, Kida, and Smith 2002) increasingly acknowledge the relevance of mood and emotional states on decision making. Generally, mood is described as being of a relatively long duration and without a single discrete identifiable antecedent cause (Moreno et al. 2002), whereas emotions are a product of both pre-existing mood and an identifiable cause (Forgas 1992). Thus, we can image a continuum from short-term task-related emotion to more enduring affective mood (Fiske and Taylor 1991; Stone and Kadous 1997).

"Irrational" personal dimensions could affect rational decision making not only in a negative but also in a positive way. Cianci and Bierstaker (2009) test the impact of an auditor's mood on her judgement. Results show that auditors in a negative mood made less ethical judgements, whereas the same mood has a positive effect on hypothesis generation performance. Concerning ethical judgements, theoretical accounting work by Gaudine and Thorne (2001) suggests that positive mood led to more ethical decisions. Lowe and Reckers (2012) examine whether specific dispositional affect states influence subordinates to acquiesce or resist ethical pressures of their superiors, finding experimental significant results.

The impact of an auditor's mood and emotional states on her performance may be moderated by other auditor characteristics. As an example, Bhattacharjee and Moreno (2002) study whether the presence of irrelevant information impacts an auditor's professional judgements, considering auditors with different experience levels. Experimental results show an effect only for the less-experienced auditors.

Conclusions

Studies examining the auditor attributes that could affect audit outcomes and auditors' judgement are growing, especially with reference to the non-JDM archival ones. Indeed, whether JDM research focusing on individual auditor judgements' determinants has a long tradition, archival non-JDM research on the topic is still in its infancy. Data availability is one of the main issues for this type of research. The possibility to have access to data on individual auditors (e.g. partner signature at the end of an audit report) is a quite recent phenomenon in most settings, whereas till now the use for research purposes of proprietary data from accounting firms and regulators is very limited. As suggested by Francis (2011: 146) greater openness from the practice to give academics access to their proprietary data is of utmost importance in order to "move beyond our current knowledge and to more fully understand and ultimately to improve audit quality." In addition, "Big Data" availability is likely to have an impact also on audit research (Vasarhelyi, Kogan, and Tuttle 2015).

Looking at the methodology approaches employed by previous literature, JDM research mainly relies on experimental methods. Experimental design allows stronger casual inference in comparison to archival research, however the possibility to replicate the experimental findings across different settings or populations has been questioned. Available non-JDM archival research is almost exclusively focused on partners and their demographic traits, due to data constrains. It is a clear limit, as former literature has documented that both other individual characteristics matter and auditors' judgements may be differentiated in dependence to their professional roles (e.g. Choo and Trotman 1991). Thus, it is of utmost importance to triangulate the results of both types of research as they complement each other's.

Also, the generalizability of the results obtained by archival studies could be problematic. Indeed, archival research mainly focused on partner attributes generally does not control for the concurrent effects of accounting firms or audit engagement offices. A notable exception is Gul et al. (2013), who propose only explorative analyses on individual partner's characteristics, as their focus is to document that a partner effect exists over and above audit firm and office effect. Moreover, previous archival researchers mainly used evidence based on audit of public companies, notwithstanding in some cases they also explored private companies in different countries around the world. From a theoretical point of view, the incentives for auditors to do a proper job are different in these two settings (i.e. audit of public and private companies). Statutory audits of private companies share some characteristics with public company audit, but "are not like financial statement audits for public companies" (Kinney 2005: 1). First, financial reporting quality cannot be assumed as homogeneous between public and private companies (e.g. Ball and Shivakumar 2005; Burgstahler, Hail, and Leuz 2006).[17] Second, previous research also shows that even considering only public companies, auditor's incentives change as investor protection regimes become stricter, due to greater likelihood that client misreporting is detected and auditors are punished (Francis and Wang 2008).

Thus, more research is needed in order to provide more insight on the individual characteristics affecting auditors' judgements and audit outcomes and overcome the abovementioned limits.

Reviewing the extant literature, it emerges that some of the relevant characteristics in explaining auditors' performances are almost partially innate, thus cannot be significantly changed over the auditor life. From the perspective of the quality of auditors' judgements and outcomes, they should be carefully considered in the selection of new entrants into the profession. At the same time, audit firms and professional bodies could undertake appropriate actions in order to reinforce other impactful individual attributes such as auditor expertise as well as organizational and environmental conditions associated with better auditors' judgements and better audit outcomes.

Overall, previous literature on the impact of individual characteristics on auditors' performance assumes that the quality of the audit being undertaken by a team depends on the sum of the skills and personality of individuals (Nelson and Tan 2005; Gul et al. 2013). However, individual choices explicitly consider other actor(s)' behaviour (Birnberg 2011). Individual auditors do not work in isolation; they are affected by their interaction within the auditing teams in which they operate as well as with other audit firms' and clients' employees/representatives. Moreover, auditors' individual goals play a relevant role. If it is clear that auditors pursue a variety of goals that, alone and in combination, influence the quality of their decisions, how the different kinds of conscious and unconscious goals affect – separately and in combination – audit judgements is still an open question (Griffith, Kadous, and Young 2016). Thus, if on one side the audit firms could consider the evidence emerging from the research summarized in this chapter for composing their teams, on the other side, the results of single-person studies often are not generalizable to multiperson settings (Trotman et al. 2015).

Audit team structures and dynamics are explicitly examined in the following chapter.

Notes

1 This Directive deals with the conditions for the approval and registration of persons that carry out statutory audits, including the rules on independence, objectivity, and professional ethics applying to them, and the framework for their public oversight. Available at http://eur-lex.europa.eu/legal-content/EN/TXT/PDF/?uri=CELEX:32006L0043&from=EN

2 IAESB is one of the several independent standard-setting boards operating under the IFAC (International Federation of Accountants) umbrella. IFAC is composed of representatives from 130 countries and jurisdictions, representing approximately 2.84 million accountants (IFAC 2016). "The aim of the IAESB is to serve the public interest by strengthening the professionalism of accountants, since recent economic events have demonstrated that questionable behaviors of the latter affect everyone, even those who do not have any direct involvement with these professionals" (Cameran and Campa 2016, p. 296). To achieve this, the IAESB mainly focuses on the development and the enhancement of accountants' education, where the latter includes both pre-qualification education and training of perspective accountants and continuing education for members of the accountancy profession. In order to achieve its mission, the IAESB issues different types of publications, including authoritative standards for IFAC members in the area of professional accounting education, named IESs (International Education Standards). In particular, IES 8 deals with "Competence Requirements for Audit Professionals". Available at https://www.ifac.org/publications-resources/ies-8-professional-competence-engagement-partners-responsible-audits-financ-0

3 A number of countries, such as Australia, China, and Taiwan, have required the disclosure of signing partners, and the European Union's Eight Directive of 2006 requires disclosure, although the requirement must be implemented separately by each member country. Some European countries had their own disclosure rules prior to the EU's Eight Directive, e.g. France, Germany, Luxembourg (Carcello and Li 2013: 1515) and Italy. In 2015 PCAOB (2015) notes that of the twenty countries with the largest stock market capitalization, only the United States, Canada, Korea, and Hong Kong do not require partner disclosure. The PCAOB recently mandated engagement partner disclosure for audit reports issued on or after January 31, 2017 (PCAOB 2015).

4 Regarding this, Francis calls for making private data available for research purposes. In fact, "further progress [in auditing research] will be best achieved through collaborative research among scholars, firms, and regulators, and this collaboration would ideally include private data from accounting firms and regulators that are needed to move beyond our current knowledge and to more fully understand and ultimately to improve audit quality" (Francis 2011: 146).

5 More recently, a working paper by Cameran, Campa, and Francis (2017) documents that also in a setting very different from the Chinese one examined by

Gul et al. (2013), that is the UK one, partner fixed effects explain more of the variation of the audit outcomes than the combined fixed effects of audit firms and audit offices.

6 Many studies have documented systematic differences between audit firms based on size (small versus large) and the firm's level of industry expertise (e.g. Craswell, Francis, and Taylor 1995; DeFond, Francis, and Wong 2000; Francis and Krishnan 1999). Other studies find evidence that individual office characteristics (e.g. engagement office size and the office's city-specific industry expertise) are important in explaining audit outcomes (e.g. Basioudis and Francis 2007; Choi, Kim, Kim, and Zang 2010; Ferguson et al. 2003; Francis, Reichelt, and Wang 2005; Francis and Yu 2009).

7 Nelson and Tan (2005) include in JDM research related to auditor and her attributes four topics: auditor knowledge and expertise, other individual characteristics, cognitive limitations, and decision aids designed to supplement or make good some deficiency in an auditor attribute, thus improving auditor performance.

8 GCOs issuance is considered a direct measure of audit quality. Indeed, it is completely under the control of the auditor and it is an extremely important output of the engagement. Moreover, GCOs issuance is also the result of both the auditor ability to detect violations and her independence (DeFond and Zhang 2014; Krishnan 1994). A higher level of GCOs indicates higher audit quality.

9 International Education Standard (IES) 1: "Entry Requirements to Professional Accounting Education Programs (Revised)", retrieved from https://www. ifac.org/publications-resources/international-education-standard-ies-1-entry-requirements-professional-accoun

10 International Accounting Standard (IES) 8: "Competence Requirements for Audit Professionals (Revised)". Available at https://www.ifac.org/publications-resources/ies-8-professional-competence-engagement-partners-responsible-audits-financ-0

11 The impact of continuous education requirement for the professionals as well as of audit companies' educational training are not explicitly considered in this chapter.

12 Some authors do not consider the audit partner tenure as an individual auditor, but as an engagement attribute. "Audit partner tenure for a particular company is not a personal characteristic of the partner; rather, it is an engagement characteristic" (Cahan and Sun 2014: 79).

13 DeAngelo (1981) defined audit quality as the probability that (a) the auditor will uncover a breach and (b) report the breach. Thus, audit quality depends both on auditor competence and her independence.

14 "Revision of the Commission's Auditor Independence Requirements", effective since February 5, 2001. Available at https://www.sec.gov/rules/final/33–7919. htm

15 Article 22.2 "Independence and objectivity" Effective since May 17, 2006. Available at http://eur-lex.europa.eu/legal-content/EN/TXT/PDF/?uri=CELEX :32006L0043&from=EN

16 Previous literature identifies two components of the auditor independence: independence in appearance and in fact. The former indicates that the auditor is perceived as being independent, whereas the latter indicates that the auditor has an independent mindset when planning and executing an audit (Dopuch, King, and Schwartz 2003).

17 This is supported by two different hypotheses (Givoly, Hayn, and Katz 2010). The "demand" argument postulates that due to stronger demand by shareholders and creditors for high-quality reporting, earnings of public firms are of higher quality. In contrast, the opportunistic behaviour posits that public company managers have a greater incentive to manage earnings. This is both due to the investors' pressure to meet certain performance benchmarks and it is the result of managers having stock-based compensation/ownership.

References

Abdolmohammadi, M., and Wright, A. (1987) An examination of the effects of experience and task complexity on audit judgments. *The Accounting Review, 62*(1), 1–13.

Alissa, W., Capkun, V., Jeanjean, T., and Suca, N. (2014) An empirical investigation of the impact of audit and auditor characteristics on auditor performance. *Accounting, Organizations and Society, 39*(7), 495–510.

Amir, E., Kallunki, J. P., and Nilsson, H. (2014) The association between individual audit partners' risk preferences and the composition of their client portfolios. *Review of Accounting Studies, 19*(1), 103–133.

Anderson, B. H., and Maletta, M. (1994) Auditor attendance to negative and positive information: The effect of experience-related differences. *Behavioral Research in Accounting, 6*, 1–20.

Aobdia, D., Lin, C. J., and Petacchi, R. (2015) Capital market consequences of audit partner quality. *The Accounting Review, 90*(6), 2143–2176.

Arnold, D. F., Bernardi, R. A., and Neidermeyer, P. E. (2001) The association between European materiality estimates and client integrity, national culture, and litigation. *The International Journal of Accounting, 36*(4), 459–483.

Arnold, D. F., Bernardi, R. A., Neidermeyer, P. E., and Schmee, J. (2007) The effect of country and culture on perceptions of appropriate ethical actions prescribed by codes of conduct: A Western European perspective among accountants. *Journal of Business Ethics, 70*(4), 327–340.

Asare, S. K., Trompeter, G. M., and Wright, A. M. (2000) The effect of accountability and time budgets on auditors' testing strategies. *Contemporary Accounting Research, 17*(4), 539–560.

Ashforth, B. E., Harrison, S. H., and Corley, K. G. (2008) Identification in organizations: An examination of four fundamental questions. *Journal of Management, 34*(3), 325–374.

Ashforth, B. E., and Mael, F. (1989) Social identity theory and the organization. *Academy of Management Review, 14*(1), 20–39.

Ashton, A. H. (1991) Experience and error frequency knowledge as potential determinants of audit expertise. *The Accounting Review, 66*(2) 218–239.

Azizkhani, M., Monroe, G. S., and Shailer, G. (2013) Audit partner tenure and cost of equity capital. *Auditing: A Journal of Practice & Theory, 32*(1), 183–202.

Baber, W. R., Krishnan, J., and Zhang, Y. (2014) Investor perceptions of the earnings quality consequences of hiring an affiliated auditor. *Review of Accounting Studies, 19*(1), 69–102.

Bailey, W., and A. Spicer. (2007) When does national identity matter? Convergence and divergence in international business ethics. *Academy of Management Journal*, *50*(6), 1462–1480.

Ball, R., and Shivakumar, L. (2005) Earnings quality in UK private firms: Comparative loss recognition timeliness. *Journal of Accounting and Economics*, *39*(1), 83–128.

Bamber, E. M., and Iyer, V. M. (2007) Auditors' identification with their clients and its effect on auditors' objectivity. *Auditing: A Journal of Practice & Theory*, *26*(2), 1–24.

Basioudis, I., and J. Francis. (2007) Audit pricing in the United Kingdom: Tests of Big 4 audit fee premia for brand name, industry leadership and city leadership. *Auditing: A Journal of Practice & Theory*, *26*(2):143–166.

Bauer, T. D. (2015) The effects of client identity strength and professional identity salience on auditor judgments. *The Accounting Review*, *90*(1), 95–114.

Bedard, J. C., and Biggs, S. F. (1991) Pattern recognition, hypotheses generation, and auditor performance in an analytical task. *The Accounting Review*, *66*(3), 622–642.

Bedard, J. C., Chi, M. T., Graham, L. E., and Shanteau, J. (1993) Expertise in auditing: Discussion. *Auditing: A Journal of Practice & Theory*, *12*(supplement), 21–45.

Bedard, J. C., and Johnstone, K. M. (2010) Audit partner tenure and audit planning and pricing. *Auditing: A Journal of Practice & Theory*, *29*(2), 45–70.

Bem, D. J., and Allen, A. (1974) On predicting some of the people some of the time: The search for cross-situational consistencies in behavior. *Psychological Review*, *81*(6), 506.

Bernardi, R. A. (1994) Fraud detection: The effect of client integrity and competence and auditor cognitive style. *Auditing: A Journal of Practice & Theory*, *13*(supplement), 68–84.

Bernardi, R. A., and Arnold, D. F. (1997) An examination of moral development within public accounting by gender, staff level, and firm. *Contemporary Accounting Research*, *14*(4), 653–668.

Bernardi, R. A., and Arnold, D. F. (2004) Testing the "Inverted-U" phenomenon in moral development on recently promoted senior managers and partners. *Contemporary Accounting Research*, *21*(2), 353–367.

Bhattacharjee, S., and Moreno, K. (2002) The impact of affective information on the professional judgments of more experienced and less experienced auditors. *Journal of Behavioral Decision Making*, *15*(4), 361–377.

Bierstaker, J. L., and Wright, S. (2001) A research note concerning practical problem-solving ability as a predictor of performance in auditing tasks. *Behavioral Research in Accounting*, *13*(1), 49–62.

Birnberg, J. G. (2011) A proposed framework for behavioral accounting research. *Behavioral Research in Accounting*, 23(1), 1–43.

Bonner, S. E. (1990) Experience effects in auditing: The role of task-specific knowledge. *The Accounting Review*, *65*(1), 72–92.

Bonner, S. E., and Lewis, B. L. (1990) Determinants of auditor expertise. *Journal of Accounting Research*, *28*, 1–20.

Bonner, S. E., and Walker, P. L. (1994) The effects of instruction and experience on the acquisition of auditing knowledge. *The Accounting Review*, *69*(1), 157–178.

Brazel, J. F., Agoglia, C. P., and Hatfield, R. C. (2004) Electronic versus face-to-face review: The effects of alternative forms of review on auditors' performance. *The Accounting Review*, *79*(4), 949–966.

Brown-Liburd, H. L., Cohen, J., and Trompeter, G. (2013) Effects of earnings forecasts and heightened professional skepticism on the outcomes of client – auditor negotiation. *Journal of Business Ethics*, *116*(2), 311–325.

Bruynseels, L., and Cardinaels, E. (2013) The audit committee: Management watchdog or personal friend of the CEO? *The Accounting Review*, *89*(1), 113–145.

Bryant, S., Murthy, U., and Wheeler, P. (2009) The effects of cognitive style and feedback type on performance in an internal control task. *Behavioral Research in Accounting*, *21*(1), 37–58.

Burgstahler, D. C., Hail, L., and Leuz, C. (2006) The importance of reporting incentives: Earnings management in European private and public firms. *The Accounting Review*, *81*(5), 983–1016.

Byrnes, J. P., Miller, D. C., and Schafer, W. D. (1999) Gender differences in risk taking: A meta-analysis. *Psychological Bulletin*, *125*(3), 367.

Cahan, S. F., Jeter, D. C., and Naiker, V. (2011) Are all industry specialist auditors the same? *Auditing: A Journal of Practice & Theory*, *30*(4), 191–222.

Cahan, S. F., and Sun, J. (2014) The effect of audit experience on audit fees and audit quality. *Journal of Accounting, Auditing & Finance*, *30*(1), 78–100.

Cameran, M. and Campa, D. (2016) Comments by the European accounting association on the international accounting education standards board consultation paper "meeting future expectations of professional competence: A consultation on the IAESB's future strategy and priorities". *Accounting in Europe*, *13*(2), 295–303.

Cameran, M., Campa, D., and Francis, J. R. (2017) How Important Is Partner Variation in Explaining Audit Quality? *Working Paper*.

Campbell, D. T., and Stanley, J. C. (1967) *Experimental and Quasi-Experimental Designs for Research*. Helsinki: Ravenio Books.

Carcello, J. V., and Li, C. (2013) Costs and benefits of requiring an engagement partner signature: Recent experience in the United Kingdom. *The Accounting Review*, 88(5), 1511–1546. doi: http://dx.doi.org/10.2308/accr-50450

Carcello, J. V., and Santore, R. (2015) Engagement partner identification: A theoretical analysis. *Accounting Horizons*, *29*(2), 297–311.

Carey, P., and Simnett, R. (2006) Audit partner tenure and audit quality. *The Accounting Review*, *81*(3), 653–676.

Casey, C. J. (1980) The usefulness of accounting ratios for subjects' predictions of corporate failure: Replication and extensions. *Journal of Accounting Research*, *18*(2), 603–613.

Chen, C. Y., Lin, C. J., and Lin, Y. C. (2008) Audit partner tenure, audit firm tenure, and discretionary accruals: Does long auditor tenure impair earnings quality? *Contemporary Accounting Research*, *25*(2), 415–445.

Chen, F., Peng, S., Xue, S., Yang, Z., and Ye, F. (2016) Do audit clients successfully engage in opinion shopping? Partner-level evidence. *Journal of Accounting Research*, *54*(1), 79–112.

Chi, H. Y., and Chin, C. L. (2011) Firm versus partner measures of auditor industry expertise and effects on auditor quality. *Auditing: A Journal of Practice & Theory*, *30*(2), 201–229.

Chi, W., Huang, H., Liao, H., and Xie, H. (2009) Mandatory audit partner rotation, audit quality, and market perception: Evidence from Taiwan. *Contemporary Accounting Research, 26*(2), 359–391.

Chin, C. L., and Chi, H. Y. (2009) Reducing restatements with increased industry expertise. *Contemporary Accounting Research*, 26(3), 729–765.

Choi, J., Kim, C., Kim, J., and Zang, Y. (2010) Audit office size, audit quality, and audit pricing. *Auditing: A Journal of Practice & Theory, 29*(1), 73–97.

Choo, F., and Tan, K. (2000) Instruction, skepticism, and accounting students' ability to detect frauds in auditing. *The Journal of Business Education, 1*, 72–87.

Choo, F., and Trotman, K. T. (1991) The relationship between knowledge structure and judgments for experienced and inexperienced auditors. *The Accounting Review, 66*(3), 464–485.

Chung, J., and Monroe, G. S. (2001) A research note on the effects of gender and task complexity on an audit judgment. *Behavioral Research in Accounting, 13*(1), 111–125.

Cianci, A. M., and Bierstaker, J. L. (2009) The impact of positive and negative mood on the hypothesis generation and ethical judgments of auditors. *Auditing: A Journal of Practice & Theory, 28*(2), 119–144.

Cohen, L., Frazzini, A., and Malloy, C. (2010) Sell-side school ties. *The Journal of Finance, 65*(4), 1409–1437.

Cohen, J. R., Pant, L. W., and Sharp, D. J. (1995) An exploratory examination of international differences in auditors' ethical perceptions. *Behavioral Research in Accounting, 7*(1), 37–64.

Cohen, J. R., and Trompeter, G. M. (1998) An examination of factors affecting audit practice development. *Contemporary Accounting Research, 15*(4), 481–504.

Coram, P., Ng, J., and Woodliff, D. R. (2004) The effect of risk of misstatement on the propensity to commit reduced audit quality acts under time budget pressure. *Auditing: A Journal of Practice & Theory, 23*(2), 159–167.

Cordes, C. L., and Dougherty, T. W. (1993) A review and an integration of research on job burnout. *Academy of Management Review, 18*(4), 621–656.

Craswell, A., Francis, J., and Taylor, S. (1995) Auditor brand name reputations and industry specializations. *Journal of Accounting and Economics, 20*(3), 297–322.

Croson, R., and Gneezy, U. (2009) Gender differences in preferences. *Journal of Economic Literature, 47*(2), 448–474.

Dalton, D. W., Buchheit, S., and McMillan, J. J. (2014) Audit and tax career paths in public accounting: An analysis of student and professional perceptions. *Accounting Horizons, 28*(2), 213–231.

DeAngelo, L. E. (1981) Auditor size and audit quality. *Journal of Accounting and Economics, 3*(3), 183–199.

DeFond, M. L., and Francis, J. R. (2005) Audit research after Sarbanes-Oxley. *Auditing: A Journal of Practice & Theory, 24*(supplement 1), 5–30.

DeFond, M. L., Francis, J., and Wong, T. (2000) Auditor industry specialization and market segmentation: Evidence from Hong Kong. *Auditing: A Journal of Practice & Theory, 19*(1), 49–66.

DeFond, M. L., and Zhang, J. (2014) A review of archival auditing research. *Journal of Accounting and Economics, 58*(2), 275–326.

DeZoort, T., Harrison, P., and Taylor, M. (2006) Accountability and auditors' materiality judgments: The effects of differential pressure strength on conservatism, variability, and effort. *Accounting, Organizations and Society*, *31*(4), 373–390.

Dobbins, G. H., Lane, I. M., and Steiner, D. D. (1988) A note on the role of laboratory methodologies in applied behavioural research: Don't throw out the baby with the bath water. *Journal of Organizational Behavior*, *9*(3), 281–286.

Dopuch, N., King, R. R., and Schwartz, R. (2003) Independence in appearance and in fact: An experimental investigation. *Contemporary Accounting Research*, *20*(1), 79–114.

Estes, R., and Reames, D. D. (1988) Effects of personal characteristics on materiality decisions: A multivariate analysis. *Accounting and Business Research*, *18*(72), 291–296.

Ferguson, A., Francis, J., and Stokes, D. (2003) The effects of firm-wide and office-level industry expertise on audit pricing. *The Accounting Review*, *78*(2), 429–448.

Finucane, M. L., Alhakami, A., Slovic, P., and Johnson, S. M. (2000) The affect heuristic in judgments of risks and benefits. *Journal of Behavioral Decision Making*, *13*(1), 1.

Firth, M., Rui, O. M., and Wu, X. (2012) How do various forms of auditor rotation affect audit quality? Evidence from China. *The International Journal of Accounting*, *47*(1), 109–138.

Fiske, S. T., and Taylor, S. E. (1991) *Social Cognition*. 2nd ed. New York: McGraw-Hill.

Forgas, J. P. (1992) Affect in social judgments and decisions: A multi-process model, in: M. Zanna, ed., *Advances in Experimental Social Psychology*. San Diego, CA: Academic Press.

Fracassi, C., and Tate, G. (2012) External networking and internal firm governance. *The Journal of Finance*, *67*(1), 153–194.

Francis, J. R. (2011) A framework for understanding and researching audit quality. *Auditing: A Journal of Practice & Theory*, *30*(2), 125–152.

Francis, J. R., and Krishnan, J. (1999) Accounting accruals and auditor reporting conservatism. *Contemporary Accounting Research*, *16*(1), 135–165.

Francis, J. R., Reichelt, K. R., and Wang, D. (2005) The pricing of national and city-specific reputations for industry expertise in the U.S. audit market. *The Accounting Review*, *80*(1), 113–136.

Francis, J. R. and Wang, D. (2008) The joint effect of investor protection and Big 4 audits on earnings quality around the world. *Contemporary Accounting Research*, *25*(1), 157–191.

Francis, J. R., and Yu, M. (2009) Big four office size and audit quality. *The Accounting Review*, *84*(5), 1521–1552.

Frederick, D. M., Heiman-Hoffman, V. B., and Libby, R. (1994) The structure of auditors' knowledge of financial statement errors. *Auditing: A Journal of Practice & Theory*, *13*(1), 1–21.

Fuller, L. R., and Kaplan, S. E. (2004) A note about the effect of auditor cognitive style on task performance. *Behavioral Research in Accounting*, *16*(1), 131–143.

Gaudine, A., and Thorne, L. (2001) Emotion and ethical decision-making in organizations. *Journal of Business Ethics*, *31*(2), 175–187.

Geiger, M. A., Lennox, C. S., and North, D. S. (2008) The hiring of accounting and finance officers from audit firms: How did the market react? *Review of Accounting Studies*, *13*(1), 55–86.

Gibbins, M., and Swieringa, R. J. (1995) Twenty years of judgment research in accounting and auditing, in: R. H. Ashton and A. H. Ashton, eds., *Judgment and Decision-Making Research in Accounting and Auditing*, 231–249. New York: Cambridge University Press.

Givoly, D., Hayn, C. K., and Katz, S. P. (2010) Does public ownership of equity improve earnings quality? *The Accounting Review*, *85*(1), 195–225.

Goodwin, J., and Wu, D. (2014) Is the effect of industry expertise on audit pricing an office-level or a partner-level phenomenon? *Review of Accounting Studies*, *19*(4), 1532–1578.

Goodwin, J., and Wu, D. (2016) What is the relationship between audit partner busyness and audit quality? *Contemporary Accounting Research*, *33*(1), 341–377.

Gordon, M. E., Slade, L. A., and Schmitt, N. (1986) The "science of the sophomore" revisited: From conjecture to empiricism. *Academy of Management Review*, *11*(1), 191–207.

Greenberg, J., and Tomlinson, E. C. (2004) Situated experiments in organizations: Transplanting the lab to the field. *Journal of Management*, *30*(5), 703–724.

Griffin, R., and Kacmar, K. M. (1991) Laboratory research in management: Misconceptions and missed opportunities. *Journal of Organizational Behavior*, *12*(4), 301–311.

Griffith, E. E., Kadous, K., and Young, D. (2016) How Insights from the "new" JDM research can improve auditor judgment: Fundamental research questions and methodological advice. *Auditing: A Journal of Practice & Theory*, *35*(2), 1–22.

Guan, Y., Su, L. N., Wu, D., and Yang, Z. (2015) Do school ties between auditors and client executives influence audit outcomes? *Journal of Accounting and Economics*, *61*(3), 506–525.

Gul, F., Wu, D., and Yang, Z. (2013) Do individual auditors affect audit quality? Evidence from archival data. *The Accounting Review*, *88*(6), 1993–2023.

Hammersley, J. S. (2006) Pattern identification and industry-specialist auditors. *The Accounting Review*, *81*(2), 309–336.

Hardies, K., Breesch, D., and Branson, J. (2015) The female audit fee premium. *Auditing: A Journal of Practice and Theory*, *34*(4), 171–195.

Hardies, K., Breesch, D., and Branson, J. (2016) Do (fe)male auditors impair audit quality? Evidence from going-concern opinions. *European Accounting Review*, *25*(1), 7–34.

Ho, J. L., and Rodgers, W. (1993) A review of accounting research on cognitive characteristics. *Journal of Accounting Literature*, *12*, 101.

Hoffman, V. B., and Patton, J. M. (1997) Accountability, the dilution effect, and conservatism in auditors' fraud judgments. *Journal of Accounting Research*, *35*(2), 227–237.

Hofstede, G. (1983) The cultural relativity of organizational practices and theories. *Journal of International Business Studies*, *14*(2), 75–89.

Holmström, B. (1999) Managerial incentive problems: A dynamic perspective. *The Review of Economic Studies*, *66*(1), 169–182.

Hong, Y. Y., Morris, M. W., Chiu, C. Y., and Benet-Martinez, V. (2000) Multicultural minds: A dynamic constructivist approach to culture and cognition. *American Psychologist, 55*(7), 709.

House, R. J., Hanges, P. J., Javidan, M., Dorfman, P. W., and Gupta, V. (2004) *Culture, Leadership, and Organizations: The GLOBE Study of 62 Societies*. Thousand Oaks, CA: Sage publications.

Hsieh, Y. T., and Lin, C. J. (2016) Audit firms' client acceptance decisions: Does partner-level industry expertise matter? *Auditing: A Journal of Practice & Theory, 35*(2), 97–120.

Hurtt, R. K. (2010) Development of a scale to measure professional skepticism. *Auditing: A Journal of Practice & Theory, 29*(1), 149–171.

IFAC. (2016) *Charting the Future Global Profession*. Retrieved from www.ifac.org/system/files/publications/files/IFAC-Strategy-for-2016-2018.pdf

Ittonen, K., Johnstone, K., and Myllymäki, E. R. (2015) Audit partner public-client specialisation and client abnormal accruals. *European Accounting Review, 24*(3), 607–633.

Ittonen, K., and Peni, E. (2012) Auditor's gender and audit fees. *International Journal of Auditing, 16*(1), 1–18.

Ittonen, K., Vähämaa, E., and Vähämaa, S. (2013) Female auditors and accruals quality. *Accounting Horizons, 27*(2), 205–228.

Jones III, A., Norman, C. S., and Wier, B. (2010) Healthy lifestyle as a coping mechanism for role stress in public accounting. *Behavioral Research in Accounting, 22*(1), 21–41.

Jones, J., Massey, D. W., and Thorne, L. (2003) Auditors' ethical reasoning: Insights from past research and implications for the future. *Journal of Accounting Literature, 22*, 45–103.

Jonnergård, K., Stafsudd, A., and Elg, U. (2010) Performance evaluations as gender barriers in professional organizations: A study of auditing firms. *Gender, Work & Organization, 17*(6), 721–747.

Jung, C. G. (1921) *Psychological Types, Collected Works*. Vol. 6. Princeton, NJ: Princeton University Press.

Karjalainen, J. (2011) Audit quality and cost of debt capital for private firms: Evidence from Finland. *International Journal of Auditing, 15*(1), 88–108.

Kelley, T., and Margheim, L. (1990) The impact of time budget pressure, personality, and leadership variables on dysfunctional auditor behavior. *Auditing: A Journal of Practice & Theory, 9*(2), 21–42.

Kennedy, J. (1993) Debiasing audit judgment with accountability: A framework and experimental results. *Journal of Accounting Research, 31*(2), 231–245.

Kennedy, J., and Peecher, M. E. (1997) Judging auditors' technical knowledge. *Journal of Accounting Research, 35*(2), 279–293.

Kida, T., and Smith, J. F. (1995) The encoding and retrieval of numerical data for decision making in accounting contexts: Model development. Accounting, *Organizations and Society, 20*(7), 585–610.

Kinney Jr, W. R. (2005) Twenty-five years of audit deregulation and re-regulation: What does it mean for 2005 and beyond? *Auditing: A Journal of Practice & Theory, 24*(supplement 1), 89–109.

Knechel, W. R., Krishnan, G. V., Pevzner, M., Shefchik, L. B., and Velury, U. K. (2013) Audit quality: Insights from the academic literature. *Auditing: A Journal of Practice & Theory*, *32*(supplement 1), 385–421.

Knechel, R. W., Vanstraelen, A., and Zerni, M. (2015) Does the identity of engagement partners matter? An analysis of audit partner reporting decisions. *Contemporary Accounting Research*, *32*(4), 1443–1478.

Kohlberg, L., and Kramer, R. (1969) Continuities and discontinuities in childhood and adult moral development. *Human Development*, *12*(2), 93–120.

Krishnan, J. (1994) Auditor switching and conservatism. *The Accounting Review*, *69*, 200–215.

Lehmann, C. M., and Norman, C. S. (2006) The effects of experience on complex problem representation and judgment in auditing: An experimental investigation. *Behavioral Research in Accounting*, *18*(1), 65–83.

Lennox, C. S. (2005) Audit quality and executive officers' affiliations with CPA firms. *Journal of Accounting and Economics*, *39*(2), 201–231.

Lennox, C. S., and Park, C. W. (2007) Audit firm appointments, audit firm alumni, and audit committee independence. *Contemporary Accounting Research*, *24*(1), 235–258.

Lennox, C. S., Wu, X., and Zhang, T. (2014) Does mandatory rotation of audit partners improve audit quality? *The Accounting Review*, *89*(5), 1775–1803.

Li, L., Qi, B., Tian, G., and Zhang, G. (2016) The Contagion effect of low-quality audits at the level of individual auditors. *The Accounting Review*, *92*(1), 137–163.

Libby, R. (1995) The role of knowledge and memory in audit judgment, in: R. H. Ashton and A. H. Ashton, eds., *Judgment and Decision-Making Research in Accounting and Auditing*, 176–206. New York: Cambridge University Press.

Libby, R., and Frederick, D. M. (1990) Experience and the ability to explain audit findings. *Journal of Accounting Research*, *28*(2), 348–367.

Libby, R., and Luft, J. (1993) Determinants of judgment performance in accounting settings: Ability, knowledge, motivation, and environment. *Accounting, Organizations and Society*, *18*(5), 425–450.

Libby, R., and Tan, H. T. (1994) Modeling the determinants of audit expertise. *Accounting, Organizations and Society*, *19*(8), 701–716.

Lim, C. Y., and Tan, H. T. (2010) Does auditor tenure improve audit quality? Moderating effects of industry specialization and fee dependence. *Contemporary Accounting Research*, *27*(3), 923–957.

Lin, K. Z., and Fraser, I. A. (2008) Auditors' ability to resist client pressure and culture: Perceptions in China and the United Kingdom. *Journal of International Financial Management & Accounting*, *19*(2), 161–183.

Liu, S. (2016) Does the requirement of an engagement partner signature improve financial analysts' information environment in the United Kingdom? *Review of Quantitative Finance and Accounting*, *2*, 1–19.

Low, K. Y. (2004) The effects of industry specialization on audit risk assessments and audit-planning decisions. *The Accounting Review*, *79*(1), 201–219.

Lowe, D. J., and Reckers, P. M. (2012) An examination of the contribution of dispositional affect on ethical lapses. *Journal of Business Ethics*, *111*(2), 179–193.

Malone, C. F., and Roberts, R. W. (1996) Factors associated with the incidence of reduced audit quality behaviors. *Auditing: A Journal of Practice & Theory*, *15*(2), 49.

Manry, D. L., Mock, T. J., and Turner, J. L. (2008) Does increased audit partner tenure reduce audit quality? *Journal of Accounting, Auditing & Finance*, *23*(4), 553–572.

Matthews, G., Deary, I. J., and Whiteman, M. C. (2003) *Personality Traits*. Cambridge: Cambridge University Press.

McDaniel, L. S. (1990) The effects of time pressure and audit program structure on audit performance. *Journal of Accounting Research*, *28*(2), 267–285.

McMillan, J. J., and White, R. A. (1993) Auditors' belief revisions and evidence search: The effect of hypothesis frame, confirmation bias, and professional skepticism. *The Accounting Review*, *68*(3), 443–465.

Menon, K., and Williams, D. D. (2004) Former audit partners and abnormal accruals. *The Accounting Review*, *79*(4), 1095–1118.

Messier Jr, W. F., Quilliam, W. C., Hirst, D. E., and Craig, D. (1992) The effect of accountability on judgment: Development of hypotheses for auditing. *Auditing: A Journal of Practice & Theory*, *11*(supplement), 123–138.

Milgrom, P., and Roberts, J. (1992) *Economics, Organization and Management*. New York: Prentice Hall.

Moreno, K., Kida, T., and Smith, J. F. (2002) The impact of affective reactions on risky decision making in accounting contexts. *Journal of Accounting Research*, *40*(5), 1331–1349.

Moroney, R., and Carey, P. (2011) Industry-versus task-based experience and auditor performance. *Auditing: A Journal of Practice & Theory*, *30*(2), 1–18.

Morris, M. G., and Venkatesh, V. (2000) Age differences in technology adoption decisions: Implications for a changing work force. *Personnel Psychology*, *53*(2), 375–403.

Morris, M. W., and Fu, H. (2001) How does cultures influence conflict resolution? Dynamic constructivist analysis. *Social Cognition*, *19*(3), 324–349.

Myers, I. B., McCaulley, M., Quenk, N. L., and Hammer, A. L. (1998) *MBTI Manual: A Guide to the Development and Use of the Myers-Briggs Type Indicator*. 3rd ed. Palo Alto, CA: Consulting Psychologists Press.

Nelson, M. W. (2009) A model and literature review of professional skepticism in auditing. Auditing: *A Journal of Practice & Theory*, *28*(2), 1–34.

Nelson, M. W., and Tan, H.T. (2005) Judgment and decision making research in auditing: A task, person, and interpersonal interaction perspective. *Auditing: A Journal of Practice & Theory*, *24*(supplement 1), 41–71.

Nguyen, B. D. (2012) Does the Rolodex matter? Corporate elite's small world and the effectiveness of boards of directors. *Management Science*, *58*(2), 236–252.

Nolder, C., and Riley, T. J. (2014) Effects of differences in national culture on auditors' judgments and decisions: A literature review of cross-cultural auditing studies from a judgment and decision making perspective. *Auditing: A Journal of Practice & Theory*, *33*(2), 141–164.

O'Donnell, E., and Johnson, E. N. (2001) The effects of auditor gender and task complexity on information processing efficiency. *International Journal of Auditing*, *5*(2), 91–105.

O'Donnell, E., and Prather-Kinsey, J. (2010) Nationality and differences in auditor risk assessment: A research note with experimental evidence. *Accounting, Organizations and Society*, *35*(5), 558–564.

Otley, D. T., and Pierce, B. J. (1996) Auditor time budget pressure: Consequences and antecedents. *Accounting, Auditing & Accountability Journal*, *9*(1), 31–58.

Owhoso, V. E., Messier Jr, W. F., and Lynch Jr, J. G. (2002) Error detection by industry-specialized teams during sequential audit review. *Journal of Accounting Research*, *40*(3), 883–900.

Palmer, K. N., Ziegenfuss, D. E., and Pinsker, R. E. (2004) International knowledge, skills, and abilities of auditors/accountants: Evidence from recent competency studies. *Managerial Auditing Journal*, *19*(7), 889–896.

Patel, C., Harrison, G. L., and McKinnon, J. L. (2002) Cultural influences on judgments of professional accountants in auditor – client conflict resolution. *Journal of International Financial Management & Accounting*, *13*(1), 1–31.

Peters, E., Västfjäll, D., Gärling, T., and Slovic, P. (2006) Affect and decision making: A "hot" topic. *Journal of Behavioral Decision Making*, *19*(2), 79–85.

Ponemon, L. A., and Gabhart, D. R. (1994) Ethical reasoning in the accounting and auditing professions, in: J. Rest and D. Narvaez, eds., *Moral Development in the Professions: Psychology and Applied Ethics*, 101–119. Hillsdale, NJ: Lawrence Erlbaum Associates.

Public Company Accounting Oversight Board (PCAOB). (2015) PCAOB supplemental request for comment: Rules to require disclosure of certain audit participants on a new PCAOB form. *Release No. 2015–004*. Retrieved from https://pcaobus.org/Rulemaking/Docket029/Release_2015_004.pdf

Quadackers, L., Groot, T., and Wright, A. (2014) Auditors' professional skepticism: Neutrality versus presumptive doubt. *Contemporary Accounting Research*, *31*(3), 639–657.

Raghunathan, B. (1991) Premature signing-off of audit procedures: An analysis. *Accounting Horizons*, *5*(2), 71–79.

Rest, J. R. (1979) *Development in Judgment Moral Issues*. Minneapolis, MN: University of Minnesota Press.

Rest, J. R. (1994) Background theory and research', in: J. Rest and D. Narvaez, eds., *Moral Development in the Professions*. Hillsdale, NJ: Lawrence Erlbaum Associates.

Rodgers, W., and Housel, T. J. (1987) The effects of information and cognitive processes on decision making. *Accounting and Business Research*, *18*(69), 67–74.

Schatzberg, J. W., Sevcik, G. R., Shapiro, B. P., Thorne, L., and Wallace, R. O. (2005) A reexamination of behavior in experimental audit markets: The effects of moral reasoning and economic incentives on auditor reporting and fees. *Contemporary Accounting Research*, *22*(1), 229–264.

Schmitt, D. P., Realo, A., Voracek, M., and Allik, J. (2008) Why can't a man be more like a woman? Sex differences in Big Five personality traits across 55 cultures. *Journal of Personality and Social Psychology*, *94*(1), 168.

Shaub, M. K. (1996) Trust and suspicion: The effects of situational and dispositional factors on auditors' trust of clients. *Behavioral Research in Accounting*, *8*, 154–174.

Shaub, M. K., and Lawrence, J. E. (1996) Ethics, experience and professional skepticism: A situational analysis. *Behavioral Research in Accounting*, 8(supplement), 124–157.

Shelton, S. W. (1999) The effect of experience on the use of irrelevant evidence in auditor judgment. *The Accounting Review*, 74(2), 217–224.

Simnett, R. (1996) The effect of information selection, information processing and task complexity on predictive accuracy of auditors. *Accounting, Organizations and Society*, 21(7), 699–719.

Solomon, I., Shields, M. D., and Whittington, O. R. (1999) What do industry-specialist auditors know? *Journal of Accounting Research*, 37(1), 191–208.

Spicer, A., Dunfee, T. W., and Bailey, W. J. (2004) Does national context matter in ethical decision making? An empirical test of integrative social contracts theory. *Academy of Management Journal*, 47(4), 610–620.

Stewart, J., Kent, P., and Routledge, J. (2016) The association between audit partner rotation and audit fees: Empirical evidence from the Australian market. *Auditing: A Journal of Practice & Theory*, 35(1), 181–197.

Stone, D. N., and Kadous, K. (1997) The joint effects of task-related negative affect and task difficulty in multiattribute choice. *Organizational Behavior and Human Decision Processes*, 70(2), 159–174.

Stone-Romero, E. F. (2002) The relative validity and usefulness of various empirical research designs, in: S. G. Rogelberg, ed., *Handbook of Research Methods in Industrial and Organizational Psychology*, 77–98. Malden, MA: Blackwell.

Sundgren, S., and Svanstrom, T. (2014) Auditor-in-charge characteristics and going-concern reporting. *Contemporary Accounting Research*, 31(2), 531–550.

Sweeney, B., Arnold, D., and Pierce, B. (2010) The impact of perceived ethical culture of the firm and demographic variables on auditors' ethical evaluation and intention to act decisions. *Journal of Business Ethics*, 93(4), 531–551.

Sweeney, J. T., and Summers, S. L. (2002) The effect of the busy season workload on public accountants' job burnout. *Behavioral Research in Accounting*, 14(1), 223–245.

Tan, H. T., and Kao, A. (1999) Accountability effects on auditors' performance: The influence of knowledge, problem-solving ability, and task complexity. *Journal of Accounting Research*, 37(1), 209–223.

Tan, H. T., and Libby, R. (1997) Tacit managerial versus technical knowledge as determinants of audit expertise in the field. *Journal of Accounting Research*, 35(1), 97–113.

Taylor, S. D. (2011) Does audit fee homogeneity exist? Premiums and discounts attributable to individual partners. *Auditing: A Journal of Practice & Theory*, 30(4), 249–272.

Thibodeau, J. C. (2003) The development and transferability of task knowledge. *Auditing: A Journal of Practice & Theory*, 22(1), 47–67.

Trotman, K. T., Bauer, T. D., and Humphreys, K. A. (2015) Group judgment and decision making in auditing: Past and future research. *Accounting, Organizations and Society*, 47, 56–72.

Trotman, K. T., Tan, H., and Ang, N. (2011) Fifty-year overview of judgment and decisionmaking research in accounting. *Accounting and Finance*, 51(1), 278–360.

Vasarhelyi, M. A. (1982) Academic research in accounting and auditing, in: von John C. Burton, Russel E. Palmer and Robert S. Kay, eds., *Handbook of accounting and auditing*. Retrieved from http://raw.rutgers.edu/MiklosVasarhelyi/Resume%20Articles/CHAPTERS%20IN%20BOOKS/C02.%20academic%20research%20in%20acct.pdf

Vasarhelyi, M. A., Kogan, A., and Tuttle, B. M. (2015) Big data in accounting: An overview. *Accounting Horizons*, *29*(2), 381–396.

Waller, W. S., and Felix, W. I. (1984) The auditor and learning from experience: Some conjectures. *Accounting, Organizations and Society*, *9*(3–4), 383–406.

Wang, Y., Yu, L., and Zhao, Y. (2015) The association between audit-partner quality and engagement quality: Evidence from financial report misstatements. *Auditing: A Journal of Practice & Theory*, *34*(3), 81–111.

Weber, E. U., and Morris, M. W. (2010) Culture and judgment and decision making: The constructivist turn. *Perspectives on Psychological Science*, *5*(4), 410–419.

Wheeler, P. R., Hunton, J. E., and Bryant, S. M. (2004) Accounting information systems research opportunities using personality type theory and the Myers-Briggs type indicator. *Journal of Information Systems*, *18*(1), 1–19.

Willett, C., and Page, M. (1996) A survey of time budget pressure and irregular auditing practices among newly qualified UK chartered accountants. *The British Accounting Review*, *28*(2), 101–120.

Wong, R. Y. M., and Hong, Y. Y. (2005) Dynamic influences of culture on cooperation in the prisoner's dilemma. *Psychological Science*, *16*(6), 429–434.

Wright, G. N., and Phillips, L. D. (1980) Cultural variation in probabilistic thinking: Alternative ways of dealing with uncertainty. *International Journal of Psychology*, *15*(1–4), 239–257.

Yamamura, J. H., Frakes, A. H., Sanders, D. L., and Ahn, S. K. (1996) A comparison of Japanese and US auditor decision-making behavior. *The International Journal of Accounting*, *31*(3), 347–363.

Yates, J. F., Lee, J. W., Shinotsuka, H., Patalano, A. L., and Sieck, W. R. (1998) Cross-cultural variations in probability judgment accuracy: Beyond general knowledge overconfidence? *Organizational Behavior and Human Decision Processes*, *74*(2), 89–117.

Ye, P., Carson, E., and Simnett, R. (2011) Threats to auditor independence: The impact of relationship and economic bonds. *Auditing: A Journal of Practice & Theory*, *30*(1), 121–148.

Zerni, M. (2012) Audit partner specialization and audit fees: Some evidence from Sweden. *Contemporary Accounting Research*, *29*(1), 312–340.

4   Auditing teams

Introduction

Solomon (1987) defines the audit team as a planned hierarchical assemblage of individuals, brought together for the purpose of the audit, which is characterized by task, responsibilities and decision-making allocations among the team members. Engagement audit teams are structured during audit planning, taking into account different factors, such as the characteristics of the auditee (size, complexity, risk, etc.), the different levels of seniority of the auditors required for the specific task, the level of knowledge and industry specialization required and finally organizational constraints such as timing, personnel availability and rotation rules (Ellifsen, Messier, Glover, and Prawitt 2013). In some cases, the audit may require consultations with external specialists, such as tax, IT or valuation experts. The typical engagement team is composed of a mix of professional roles (typically juniors, seniors, managers and partners) to each of whom specific tasks and responsibilities are assigned. Juniors typically have up to two years of audit experience and their duties consist of performing the audit procedures assigned to them, preparing adequate and appropriate documentation of completed work, and informing the senior about any auditing or accounting problems encountered. Seniors (2–5 years of experience) generally assist in the development of the audit plan, preparation of an audit budget, assigning audit tasks to juniors, and directing the day-to-day audit activities. Seniors also supervise and review the work of juniors and inform managers about any auditing or accounting problems encountered. Managers, with a typical audit experience of 5–10 years, ensure that the audit is properly planned, which includes scheduling of team members; reviewing the engagement working papers, the financial statements and the audit report; dealing with invoicing and ensuring collection of payment for audit services; and, finally, informing the partner about any auditing or accounting problem encountered. Partners are ultimately responsible for the audit. They reach agreement with the client on the scope of the services to be provided and ensure that the audit is properly planned and the audit team has the required skills and experience; they supervise the audit team and review the working papers; finally they sign the final audit report[1] (Ellifsen et al. 2013).

Audit team composition

According to Dereli, Baykasoğlu, and Daş (2007), the audit team is initially formed by the partner, on the basis of the auditors' skills and the needs/ expectations of the auditee. Goetsch and Davis (2002) suggest that the lead auditor should consider the following aspects when selecting audit team members:

- Competence of candidate auditors;
- The type of organization, processes, activities or functions being audited;
- The number, language skills and expertise of the auditors;
- Any potential conflict of interest between audit members and the organization being audited;
- Requirements of the audited organization, and of certification and accreditation bodies.

According to Goetsch and Davis (2002), audit teams should be characterized by a combination of auditing skills, communication skills and technical and management knowledge. The challenge, according to the authors, is to form an appropriate audit team by matching the skills of candidate auditors with the skill requirements of the audit engagement, subject to several constraints related to cost, project and human resources.

Audit standards do not require a specific audit team structure. Maister (1982), when referring to professional services in general (in which he includes audit firms), states that the relative mix of juniors, managers, and seniors depends on specific projects and is influenced by the mix of client relations activities, project management and professional tasks involved in the specific engagement, where, in the case of an audit, partners would be typically responsible for client relations, managers and seniors for the day-to-day supervision and coordination of the activity, while juniors would carry out the technical tasks necessary to complete the study. Ellifsen, Knechel, and Wallage (2001), focusing on an engagement involving a bank client in 1997, estimated that around 40 per cent of engagement hours were charged by juniors, while around 4–6 per cent of total engagement hours were charged by specialists.[2] Livatino, Pecchiari, and Pogliani (2011: 77) state that, on average, 4–7 per cent of engagement hours would be allocated to audit partners, 14–17 per cent to audit managers, 25–35 per cent to seniors and the remaining 57–41 per cent to juniors.

Audit literature has shown that even if task allocation among the different roles is not usually rigid in auditing firms (this is valid in general for professional firms, as suggested by Maister (1982), given that in a well-established audit juniors will be increasingly assigned senior tasks, and seniors will be asked to take some of the managers' responsibilities), superior audit performance requires task-specific knowledge (Ashton 1991; Bedard and Chi 1993; Abdolmohammadi 1999). In particular, audit literature distinguishes between structured and unstructured tasks. The former are defined as tasks in which the problem is well defined and the number of alternatives is limited, therefore requiring very little judgement to make the final decision. In unstructured tasks, problems are ill-defined and have many alternative solutions requiring considerable judgement and insight to make the final decision (Abdolmohammadi 1999). There are also the so-called semi-structured tasks, with a limited number of alternative solutions, requiring a medium level of judgement. Abdolmohammadi and Wright (1987) demonstrated differences in audit judgements between experienced and non-experienced auditors for unstructured and semi-structured tasks, but not for structured tasks. Ramsay (1994), focusing on review processes, demonstrates that audit managers outperform (i.e. are more accurate than) seniors in detecting conceptual errors in workpaper review, where conceptual errors are defined as subjective, unverifiable and imprecise. On the other hand, seniors outperform managers in detecting mechanical errors, defined as objective, verifiable and concrete.

Audit literature has also shown that role ambiguity, intended as uncertainty about key requirements of their tasks (Baron 1986), of audit team members is a potential threat for audit performance. Auditors are in fact typically allocated to multiple engagements and are assigned to more than one supervisor each with a different management style and directive. This potentially causes auditors to spend time and resources to try to solve this conflict, devoting fewer resources to perform their assigned duties (Fried, Ben-David, Tiegs, Avital, and Yeverechyahu 1998; Vera-Muñoz, Ho, and Chow 2006).

Audit team specialization

Recently, audit literature has given great attention to audit specialization as a critical determinant of audit quality and effectiveness. Audit team specialization is therefore considered an important characteristic when setting up an audit plan. Lindow and Race (2002), in this respect, highlight that auditors do not just audit control activities, but they also monitor companies' risk profile and play a key role in improving risk management processes. For this reason, audit teams must be able to fully understand the business risks of the company. Wooten (2003) highlights that specialization is one of the most important audit team characteristics that affect audit quality. As he states, "working on multiple clients within the same industry allows the staff to become expert in the processes and procedures unique to that industry. By understanding the common weaknesses, risks and issues faced by a particular industry, an auditor can be more confident and persistent when assessing the evidence presented by the client" (Wooten 2003: 50). Owhoso, Messier, and Lynch, (2002) demonstrate that error detection by managers and seniors improves within industry-specialized teams, while non-specialized teams are not effective at detecting both mechanical and conceptual errors. Moroney and Simnet (2009) find that complex industry specialists (for example pension fund auditors) are on average better able to list relatively more business risks when working in their industry than generic industry specialists (i.e. manufacturing auditors) are able to do in their respective industries. The authors also find that complex industry specialists, working in their industries, are able to list a greater number of appropriate information sources and appropriate evidence-gathering processes compared to their generic industry peers. Audit team specialization also has a positive impact on audit team commitment, if the audit firm takes into account the interest and career paths of its personnel (Vera-Muñoz et al. 2006). Industry specialists demonstrate a less conservative assessment of inherent risk levels (Taylor 2000), a more accurate non-error frequency knowledge (Solomon, Shields, and Whittington 1999), a more effective detection of seeded errors during the review process (Owhoso et al. 2002), a more accurate assessment of audit risk (Low 2004) and a greater ability to interpret and complete partial cue patterns (Hammersley 2006). Moroney and Carey (2011) find that industry-based experience is relatively more important than task-based experience in non-specialist auditors. It is therefore evident that industry specialization should be an important aspect to consider for audit firms when staffing the specific engagements. However, this practice is not always applied by audit firms, who have both time and cost constraints and necessarily assign audit teams to different industries, clients and projects. Muczyk, Smith, and Davis (1986) highlight that managers and even partners are often generalists, as they know the auditing process thoroughly but do not necessarily have acquired in-depth knowledge about a single industry. More often, due to the context of increasing complexity of accounting, auditors interact with external specialists; they are more frequently seeking the assistance of specialists from such fields as tax, information technology, valuations and forensic accounting (Boritz, Kochetova-Kozloski, and Robinson 2015).[3]

Audit team continuity

When deciding staff allocation of auditors across engagements, it is also important to consider past experience with the specific client, as audit team "continuity" can have a positive effect on audit quality and audit efficiency. Indeed, as time passes, learning occurs by both the auditor and the client. The auditor becomes familiar with the client, its processes, personnel and culture. The audit team can develop better and more precise skills concerning the specific industry and the organization of the specific client. Moreover, team continuity minimizes information asymmetry (Bedard and Johnstone 2010) and enhances objectivity (Udeh 2015). This learning curve, which has positive effects on the audit process, necessarily requires time. Consistent with this argument, most of the studies on the impact of audit tenure on audit quality have found that audit failures occur on average during the first years of engagement (Petty and Cuganesan 1996; Geiger and Raghunandan 2002; Myers and Omer 2003; Carcello and Nagy 2004). Team continuity is also usually positively perceived by the audit client, who can save time and resources by communicating with the same members of the audit team and who can rely on auditors' past experience.

Academics and regulators, however, have also highlighted that audit team continuity can potentially have negative impacts on audit quality and effectiveness, for two main reasons. Long audit tenures might impair audit independence due to tightening of relationships between the management and the auditor (Mautz and Sharaf 1961; Farmer, Rittenberg, and Trompeter 1987; Brody and Moscove 1998). Long-term engagements may also increase the risk of the auditor following a "professional routine" by relying excessively on previous years' control tests and becoming complacent (Shockley 1981). Auditor changes reduce this familiarity threat, as they bring in "new fresh eyes", thus increasing the auditor critical capacity (McLaren 1958; AICPA 1978; Hoyle 1978).

The team is not merely the sum of individuals

Teams are formed by individuals who can interact in different ways: supervise, advise and support each other, with the ultimate aim of providing a more effective service to clients. Teams are proven to be more effective than individuals, and different studies have attempted to deepen and empirically prove this phenomenon. Einhorn, Hogarth, and Klempner (1977), for example, show that the quality of group judgements is on average better than that of individuals and this can be explained by a reduction in the error inherent in individual judgements. If interaction between group members allows a group to act as if a member's contribution is weighted by the rank of his or her relative expertise, then error inherent in individual judgements is further reduced, resulting in a distribution that is "tighter" than the distribution of unit weight composite judgements (interaction effect). Schultz and Reckers (1981) state that the evaluation of information conducted by a group (team) seems to be much richer than non-group-assisted evaluation. The authors state that group consulting brings in more complete documentation of the decision process, no significant choice shifts, greater consistency in evaluations and increased confidence in the post-individual evaluations, supporting the view that group decision processes outperform those of individuals.

Brainstorming in audit teams

Starting from these premises, audit literature has tried to understand what are the best means to enhance audit team group performance. One of these is without a doubt brainstorming, which is also mandated by International Audit Standards (SAS 99). Brainstorming sessions are defined as "an exchange of ideas or 'brainstorming' among the audit team members about how and where they believe the entity's financial statements might be susceptible to material misstatement due to fraud and how management could perpetrate and conceal fraudulent financial reporting" (AICPA 2002). Carpenter (2007) shows empirically that brainstorming sessions on average generate more quality fraud ideas than the respective sum of individual auditors (defined as the "nominal group"), even if this comes at the cost of reducing the overall quantity of ideas. In particular, the author demonstrates that brainstorming audit teams reduce ideas that are not quality fraud ideas, and at the same time are able to produce new quality fraud ideas. Hoffman and Zimbelman (2009) focus on brainstorming sessions conducted by audit managers on planned audit activities. The authors find that after brainstorming sessions audit managers tend to modify audit procedures in a more effective way to cope with fraud cases. Given that brainstorming, besides being mandated by audit standards, seems indeed to be an effective way to enhance audit quality, the audit literature has widely studied this phenomenon, focusing on different approaches that may be implemented practically. Standard setters suggest that brainstorming sessions should be conducted face-to-face during the planning phase of the audit:[4] the team organizes a meeting and discusses (face-to face) key issues of the audit work. The face-to-face brainstorming may be "nominal" or "interacting": the first is characterized by participants who have worked alone on the task, as individuals, and at a second stage they combine the different tasks and ideas together. The latter, on the other hand, implies discussions among the team members (Trotman, Bauer, and Humphreys 2015). Early literature supported this choice, as it was believed that interacting group brainstorming increases creativity in idea generation (Osborn 1957): with this tool, the group can share a lot of different ideas and also generate new ones, through cognitive stimulation. As mentioned by Trotman et al. (2015), early psychology studies argue that nominal brainstorming on average outperforms interacting brainstorming by generating more ideas. These studies state that in interacting brainstorming, certain group mechanisms arise which lead to a loss of ideas. For example; production blocking occurs when only one group member can communicate at once, which can result in forgetting ideas, suppressing ideas, and remembering and listening, rather than creating ideas. Another example refers to evaluation apprehension where group members do not share ideas due to fear of negative evaluation. Finally, interactive brainstorming might lead to free riding when individuals tend to rely on others to complete the task as they believe their inputs are unidentifiable or dispensable (Trotman et al. 2015). As highlighted by Trotman et al. (2015), however, it should be noted that these studies generally rely on experiments conducted with students (therefore non-specialists) and results might therefore be biased by the level of task knowledge of participants. Audit team members are on the contrary experienced professionals asked to solve complex and highly technical tasks. This might also explain results by Carpenter (2007) who finds beneficial effects of interactive brainstorming.

Brainstorming can be classified, moreover, into "unstructured" and "structured". Unstructured brainstorming is a technique in which very few rules and guidelines are set down to conduct the brainstorming sessions and typically group members share ideas in an unstructured way, as they come to mind. This is the brainstorming technique usually used in practice by audit firms (Brazel, Carpenter, and Jenkins 2010). However, unstructured brainstorming sessions are proven to be not particularly effective, and can even result in a degenerating process in which the discussion is jeopardized by a few group members (Brazel et al. 2010). Trotman, Simnett, and Khalifa (2009) analyzed methods of conducting brainstorming sessions alternative to the unstructured (or "open") ones. In particular, they find that setting down specific brainstorming guidelines (based on Osborn 1957)[5] improves the quantity and quality of fraud ideas. Trotman et al. (2009) also look at the impact of including "premortem" instructions on brainstorming success. The "premortem strategy" was initially studied by Klein (1999) and consists of the use of mental simulation to find flaws in a plan. In the auditing setting, "premortem" strategy implies asking auditors to imagine a scenario where an accounting fraud was discovered for a specific client months after the audit was completed and where auditors did not highlight any material misstatement. By forcing auditors to adopt a "backward looking" approach, the authors hypothesize, and find, that brainstorming sessions with premortem instructions increase quantity and quality of fraud ideas. Electronic brainstorming leverages on information technology to enhance the effectiveness of brainstorming. In particular, group members might gather physically in one room or may connect from remote locations via an electronic link and are asked to type ideas about potential fraud risks (Beasley and Jenkins 2003) which are simultaneously seen (either on computers or on a screen) by all group members. Group discussions and consolidation of ideas is then supported by the computer software. Lynch, Murthy, and Engle (2009) empirically show that electronic brainstorming outperforms face-to-face sessions both when it is nominal and when it is interacting.[6] In particular, they show that the detection of relevant fraud risks increases in the presence of an automatic content "facilitator" that might stimulate and prompt the generation of new ideas. Another stream of literature is studying the effectiveness of strategic reasoning as a way to encourage more creative risk detection procedures. Hoffman and Zimbelman for example, define strategic reasoning as answering the following questions: "What potential frauds may have occurred? How could management conceal the potential frauds from the standard audit plan? How could the plan be modified to detect the concealed frauds?" (Hoffman and Zimbelman 2009: 812). Strategic reasoning can be applied both by auditors individually (i.e. without brainstorming) or as a combination with brainstorming sessions. The authors find that both approaches (i.e. strategic reasoning and brainstorming) when used separately (i.e. not simultaneously) lead to more effective changes in the standard audit procedures compared to audit approaches without interventions. On the other hand, the authors find that both approaches together do not provide significant additional benefits above that achieved by using just one of the interventions.

Consultation within the firm

Consultation implies the interaction among professionals when an auditor needs clarifications or opinions from a specialist or a colleague. This type of feedback activity becomes extremely important in cases in which the auditors need to defend or even document their actions within the team or before external inspectors (Emby and Gibbins 1987; Trotman et al. 2015). This process may be both formal and informal (Trotman et al. 2015). The audit literature has studied different aspects of formal consultation. A stream of research studies, for example, focus on the reasons underlying consultation perceived needs. Kennedy, Kleinmuntz, and Peecher (1997) and Emby and Gibbins (1987) affirm that consultation is a source of justification for auditors; it is believed consulting an expert auditor increases the justifiability of professionals' decisions, especially when the advice confirms the consulting auditor's initial position. The confirming advice is in fact seen as more justifiable (Kennedy et al. 1997).

However, consultation may also be informal, whereby auditors informally ask for peers' opinions. Kadous, Leiby, and Peecher (2013) state that in such situations, when the opinion asked is in contrast with the original belief of the auditor, generally auditors tend to revise in line with advice regardless of treatment (Trotman et al. 2015). Specifically, non-specialist auditors use a "trust heuristic" approach; they tend to weigh advice according to its justifiability (i.e. defensibility of the recommendation) when these come from a peer with whom they share a weaker social bond, while they are less concerned about the quality of advice received when they seek advice from a peer with whom they share strong social bonds. On the other hand, specialist auditors consider justified advice of better quality when the advisor's social bond is stronger; however, specialists discount better justified advice coming from close advisors (Kadous et al. 2013). Few papers are furthermore focusing on the relation between the informal consultation and the audit team structure and characteristics. Nelson, Proell, and Randel (2016) show that auditors are more willing to consult with audit team superiors when the latter have a more team-oriented leadership style. In particular, auditors ask for an informal consultation when there are issues concerning audit costs and increasing effectiveness.

Another stream of literature is focusing on the willingness to ask for formal consulting advice from audit specialists. Asare and Wright (2004) and Gold, Knechel, and Wallage (2012) show that auditors tend to ask for formal consultation to fraud specialists when the fraud risk is higher. However, Gold et al. (2012) specify that fraud specialists' involvement occurs more frequently when the requirement to consult is stricter, and fraud risk and engagement time pressure are higher. This is in line with literature that focuses on choice justifiability: not asking for specialists' advice when fraud risk is higher is less justifiable in the face of third parties, especially when requirements are stricter. Boritz et al. (2015) analyzed the impact of fraud specialist involvement in audit planning, and found that, on average, fraud specialists generated a greater number of non-standard additional audit procedures, which were marginally more effective, but less efficient, than those of auditors. The authors also showed that the increase in audit budget proposed by fraud specialists as a consequence of the additional (non-standard) audit procedures was significantly smaller than the budget increase proposed by auditors. Brazel and Agoglia (2007) analyzed the impact of complex accounting information system and computer assurance expertise in assessing clients' internal control risk.

Focus on professional practice and regulation

In this section audit teams are analyzed from a regulatory point of view. In particular, the role of audit teams and the requirements settled by International Standards on Auditing (ISA) will first be exposed. Then a reference to the role of audit teams in the Public Company Accounting Oversight Board (PCAOB) audit quality indicators will be made.

Second, standard audit team structure in practice is presented: audit firms are characterized by a typical team (pyramidal) structure and career path, which are described and commented on in the second part of this section.

Finally, audit firms disclosure about their approach towards audit teams is analyzed by looking at the transparency and audit quality reports and annual reviews of the Big 4 audit firms.

ISA: characteristics of an adequate engagement team

ISA highlight the importance of teams as fundamental elements of an audit process. In particular, ISA emphasize the:

(a) Importance of structuring an appropriate engagement team (ISA 1, ISA 220),
(b) Engagement team role in audit planning (ISA 300),
(c) Engagement team role in risk detecting (ISA 200), and
(d) Importance of the engagement team characteristics in the review process (ISA 220).

ISA 1 introduces the importance of building an appropriate engagement team. In this respect, in fact, it states that the firm should establish policies and procedures to assign appropriate personnel with the necessary competence and capabilities to:

(a) Perform engagements in accordance with professional standards and applicable legal and regulatory requirements, and
(b) Enable the firm or engagement partners to issue reports that are appropriate in the circumstances.

The firm's assignment of engagement teams and the determination of the level of supervision required include, for example, consideration of the engagement team's:

• Understanding of, and practical experience with, engagements of a similar nature and complexity through appropriate training and participation;
• Understanding of professional standards and applicable legal and regulatory requirements;
• Technical knowledge and expertise, including knowledge of relevant information technology;

- Knowledge of relevant industries in which the clients operate;
- Ability to apply professional judgement; and
- Understanding of the firm's quality control policies and procedures.

Moreover, ISA 220 highlights that the engagement partner should ascertain that the engagement team and the audit experts who are not part of the engagement team collectively have the appropriate competence and capabilities to:

(a) Perform the audit engagement in accordance with professional standards and applicable legal and regulatory requirements, and
(b) Enable an auditor's report that is appropriate in the circumstances to be issued.

In addition, ISA 300 affirms that, on the one hand, adequate planning benefits the audit of financial statements in several ways, including the selection of engagement team members with appropriate levels of capabilities and competence to respond to anticipated risks, and the proper assignment of work to them. On the other hand, the involvement of the engagement partner and other key members of the engagement team in planning the audit draws on their experience and insight, thereby enhancing the effectiveness and efficiency of the planning process. ISA 300 establishes, consequently, a close causal relation among the engagement team's experience, audit planning adequacy and audit quality.

A further element affected by the engagement team's characteristics, according to ISA 200, is risk detection. This objective relates, in fact, to the nature, timing and extent of the audit procedures that are determined by the auditor to reduce audit risk to an acceptably low level. It is therefore a function of the effectiveness of an audit procedure and of its application by the auditor. Matters such as:

- adequate planning,
- proper assignment of personnel to the engagement team,
- the application of professional skepticism, and
- supervision and review of the audit work performed

enhance the effectiveness of an audit procedure and of its application and reduce the possibility that an auditor might select an inappropriate audit procedure, misapply an appropriate audit procedure or misinterpret the audit results.

Concerning the appropriateness of the review process, ISA 220 states that the firm's review of responsibility policies and procedures is determined on the basis that work of less experienced team members is reviewed by more experienced team members.

PCAOB: audit quality indicators

The PCAOB provides auditing and related professional practice standards to be followed in the preparation and issuance of audit reports for registered public audit firms. On July 1, 2015, it issued the Concept Release on Audit Quality Indicators, which are measures aimed at providing new insights on audit quality. In particular, the release aimed at seeking public comments on the content and possible uses of these potential indicators. The measures proposed are reported in Table 4.1.

In particular, indicators from 1 to 10 specifically refer to the engagement team's structure and skills.

The definitions of such ratios are the following:

1 "Staffing Leverage" measures the time of experienced senior personnel relative to the volume of audit work they oversee.
2 "Partner Workload" refers to the level of work for which the audit engagement partner is responsible and the number of claims on his or her attention.
3 "Manager and Staff Workload" provides information about the workload of audit managers and audit staff.
4 "Technical Accounting and Auditing Resources" measures the level of a firm's central personnel (or other resources engaged by the firm) available to provide engagement teams with advice on complex, unusual, or unfamiliar issues and the extent to which they are used in a particular engagement.
5 "Persons with Specialized Skill and Knowledge" measures the use in an audit engagement of persons with "specialized skill and knowledge," other than accounting and auditing personnel counted as technical accounting and auditing resources under indicator 4. These individuals may be firm personnel or they may be retained by the firm.
6 "Experience of Audit Personnel" measures the level of experience of members of a particular engagement team and the weighted average experience of firm personnel generally.
7 "Industry Expertise of Audit Personnel" addresses the experience of senior members of the audit team as well as specialists in the industry in which the audited company operates.
8 "Turnover of Audit Personnel" refers to transfers to other engagements or movement to other firms at the engagement and, more generally, at the firm level.

Table 4.1 Public Company Accounting Oversight Board (PCAOB) quality indicators

AUDIT PROFES-SIONALS	*Availability*	1	Staffing Leverage
		2	Partner Workload
		3	Manager and Staff Workload
		4	Technical Accounting and Auditing Resources
		5	Persons with Specialized Skill and Knowledge
	Competence	6	Experience of Audit Personnel
		7	Industry Expertise of Audit Personnel
		8	Turnover of Audit Personnel
		9	Amount of Audit Work Centralized at Service Centers
		10	Training Hours per Audit Professional
	Focus	11	Audit Hours and Risk Areas
		12	Allocation of Audit Hours to Phases of the Audit
AUDIT PROCESS	*Tone at the Top and Leadership*	13	Results of Independent Survey of Firm Personnel
	Incentives	14	Quality Ratings and Compensation
		15	Audit Fees, Effort, and Client Risk
	Independence	16	Compliance with Independence Requirements
	Infrastructure	17	Investment in Infrastructure Supporting Quality Auditing
	Monitoring and Remediation	18	Audit Firms' Internal Quality Review Results
		19	PCAOB Inspection Results
		20	Technical Competency Testing
AUDIT RESULTS	*Financial Statements*	21	Frequency and Impact of Financial Statement Restatements for Errors
		22	Fraud and Other Financial Reporting Misconduct
		23	Inferring Audit Quality from Measures of Financial Reporting Quality
	Internal Control	24	Timely Reporting of Internal Control Weaknesses
	Going Concern	25	Timely Reporting of Going Concern Issues
	Communications between Auditors and Audit Committee	26	Results of Independent Surveys of Audit Committee Members
	Enforcement and Litigation	27	Trends in PCAOB and SEC Enforcement Proceedings
		28	Trends in Private Litigations

9 "Amount of Audit Work Centralized at Service Centers" refers to the degree to which audit work is centralized by the audit firm at service centers.

10 "Training Hours per Audit Professional" focuses on the hours of relevant training – including industry-specific training – that members of the engagement team, and of the team's firm, have received.

The work of PCAOB has been closely followed by the Center for Audit Quality (CAQ), which has elaborated its own Audit Quality Indicators proposal, which is similar to the PCAOB's project. In addition, methods and means aimed at enhancing audit quality have received increased international attention, as represented by the proliferating of reports and documents such as the International Assurance and Auditing Standards Board's Framework for Audit Quality,[7] which further highlights the central role of audit team structure in enhancing audit quality.

It is interesting to note that the topics included in these ten indicators have been further analyzed by literature, as shown in the previous paragraphs: both academics and regulators are, in conclusion, focusing on audit quality and are studying the team as a fundamental element that can enhance it.

Audit firms' approach towards team role

This section examines international audit firms' approach towards the team role. In particular, an analysis of the three different international documents published by the Big 4 on their websites is conducted. The documents considered[8] are the global report,[9] the audit quality report,[10] and the annual review.[11]

From the analysis of these documents, it appears evident that particular attention is devoted to the concept of team diversity and to personal development programs.

In particular, audit firms state that they aim at building teams with the broadest range of skills, experiences and perspectives. In order to achieve this objective, they tend to recruit students and professionals from very different backgrounds, specializations and cultures. As a result, audit firms commit themselves to the delivery of diversity programs promoting an inclusive leadership, culture and work environment. Particular attention is paid to gender equality: audit firms often report not only the total numbers of female employees but also their distribution among different seniority levels.

Personal development programs, on the other hand, are designed in order to ensure employees continuous learning and improvement. In fact, Big 4 companies recognize that their reputations are based on their ability not only to hire talented people but also to provide them with challenging professional growth. In order to achieve this objective, audit firms require, for example, the completion of different continuous learning programs for each seniority level.

Furthermore, Big 4 companies require partners and management to be responsible for the team members' growth. In order to effectively achieve this objective, these firms often support engagement teams with internal communication tools and procedures aimed at facilitating feedback and periodic evaluations. In addition, each professional is usually assigned to a more experienced counselor in order to help him or her to identify opportunities for further development.

Some extracts from the Big 4 documents follow.

KPMG: global transparency report 2015[12]

All candidates for professional positions submit an application and are employed following a variety of selection processes, which may include application screening, competency-based interviews, psychometric and ability testing, and qualification/reference checks. Upon joining a KPMG member firm new personnel are required to participate in a comprehensive on-boarding program, which includes training in areas such as ethics and independence. This also includes ensuring that any issues of independence or conflicts of interest are addressed before the individual can commence as a partner or employee with the firm. Member firm recruiting strategies are focused on drawing entry-level talent from a broad talent base, including relationships with established universities, colleges and business schools in respective countries, alongside secondary schools, enabling us to build relationships with a younger, diverse talent pool at an earlier age. . . .

It is important that all professionals have the necessary business and leadership skills to be able to perform quality work in addition to technical skills. In relation to audit, we provide opportunities for professionals to develop the skills, behaviors, and personal qualities that form the foundations of a successful career in auditing. Courses are available to enhance personal effectiveness and develop technical, leadership, and business skills. We further develop our personnel for high performance through coaching and mentoring on the job, stretch assignments, and country rotational and global mobility opportunities. . . .

We work hard to foster a diverse and inclusive culture. In doing so we are able to build teams with the broadest range of skills, experiences and perspectives – teams that then bring the most innovative ideas to clients. We believe that clients deserve the very best we can offer and this can only be achieved when we have a work environment that is inclusive, fair and ethical. We understand that our leadership and management teams also need to reflect the diversity of our organization and that we have to create inclusive leadership programs for our people to ensure we continue to be the best choice for clients. Our well established Global Diversity Network drives the changes necessary to promote inclusive leadership across KPMG's global network. We also support a number of innovative programs which research, promote and sustain a more diverse and inclusive culture and work environment. Our work with academics, for example, is finding new ways to challenge the status quo and make progress towards diversity and inclusion.

PWC: global annual review 2015[13]

Our talent strategy is designed to help our people continuously develop their leadership skills, grow their careers, and deliver consistently extraordinary results for clients. With these goals in mind, PwC US has created the Leadership Development Experience (LDE), an integrated and personalized approach to growth and development. It emphasizes real-time development through frequent, informal feedback against the dimensions of The PwC Professional – our global career progression framework – to maximize strengths, quickly close gaps and drive continuous learning. We've started to see results. In our latest Global People Survey conducted in April 2015, our US Engagement Index score was 84%, its highest ever. And in the same survey, 80% of our people said that since the LDE launched in September 2014, they have had a meaningful conversation about their development. Spotting development opportunities.

This year, the PwC Professional was brought to life by rolling out an interactive video-based simulation called The PwC Professional: Spotting Development Opportunities. An immersive, "choose-your-own adventure" experience with game-like features and immediate feedback, the simulation – which won "Gold" in the 2015 Learning & Performance Institute Awards for Innovation in Learning – lets partners and staff see what happens if they seize the learning opportunities that are all around them every day. The simulation is structured around six characters – five PwC team members and a client – and takes place over 48 hours during a critical juncture for the client. Gameplay begins when a learner enters one of the five character "worlds". . . .

I'm completely – and boldly – confident of one fact about PwC: to solve important problems we need diverse talent. That's why we employ people from a vast array of backgrounds and with an equally wide range of experiences. This means they each think differently from one another, and apply varying approaches to problem solving. And we're committed to helping every one of our people build a rewarding career and achieve their full potential.

EY: global report 2015[14]

Starting from the beginning, at recruitment, candidates learn about the issues our clients face and our purpose of building a better working world. Whether joining EY or not, they find out more about themselves through the interview process and opportunities like our intern programs around the world. The outstanding candidates who join EY participate in world-class learning, coaching, counseling and on-the-job experiences that provide opportunities to contribute, excel and build careers. We focus on creating and maintaining a diverse and inclusive environment where everybody's voices are heard and valued and where there is flexibility in how and where people work. The EY culture is an important reason why people join EY and develop their careers here. Two powerful elements of our culture are highest performing teams and a global and inclusive vision of leadership. Highest performing teams inspire individual and collective success. Across all ranks and roles, we are advancing a culture of worldclass, highest performing teams that create lasting value for us, our people and clients. Engaged and inspired by a shared vision, highest performing teams bring together the right mix of talent and deliver quality results that surpass expectations. Leadership is one of the hallmarks of the exceptional EY experience for all our people. Developing inclusive leaders underpins how we make the world work better, as the actions of EY leaders have a lasting impact on our clients, our people and our communities. Our distinctive definition of leadership at EY provides one shared vision and language of leadership to unite our efforts in building the leaders of tomorrow, for EY and for the world.

When people eventually leave EY, their lifetime experience continues. We are proud of the more than 800,000 EY alumni who today are excelling in business, government and academia and who remain connected to the EY family through our global alumni program. For every one of our people, this is how we sum it up: Whenever you join, however long you stay, the exceptional EY experience lasts a lifetime.

Deloitte: audit quality report 2015[15]

Deloitte is a recognized leader and employer of choice. We are consistently ranked as one of the best places to work and honored for our inclusive culture and diverse workforce. The reason for our success is straightforward: we invest in our people, to give them opportunities to grow and thrive. We have made substantial investments in our talent strategies and transformed our technical audit curriculum. Deloitte auditors have logged approximately 750,000 hours of learning in our updated curriculum this year alone. We target learners by level of expertise, using a dynamic mix of live, instructor led, virtual, and engagement team-based courses. We monitor extensively for compliance, and equip learners to bring lessons back to the engagement team where they can be applied to fieldwork. These efforts are already yielding strong results

A holistic approach: Audit 360° Our professional development model has become more holistic, moving beyond technical education to include industry specialization, exercises in critical thinking, and leadership development. A new learning system called Audit 360° deepens our investment in this holistic approach. Audit 360° allows all of our audit professionals to tailor both technical and soft skills curricula more closely to their needs, specify on-the-job experiences that will help them grow, and gain exposure to people and projects that will expand their professional competence. Next-generation learning:

We continue to evolve our learning platforms, leveraging innovative approaches and new technologies. Nano Learning is one area we are exploring. These bite-size lessons are delivered in 10–30 minute increments, putting critical information in professionals' hands in a timely way while also building a valuable library of readily accessible and searchable information assets. We are also exploring and piloting new analytics learning across our organization. The profession requires analytics specialists now and we anticipate the day when every auditor we recruit will have working knowledge of analytics. Learning to interpret large data sets and building a big data story will occupy an increasingly important role in professional development, and enable auditors to deliver the deeper insights today's investing public demands.

Notes

1 The actual denomination of each position varies from firm to firm, but the career path is generally similar in all audit firms. Advancements in this sector are on average quite rapid and usually promotions across levels are the consequence of a detailed valuation and feedback process, implemented by professionals of higher levels.
2 The study focuses on an audit carried out in 1997, but the percentages described did not change, according to the authors, as a result of the market pressure and evolution of audit practices that occurred in the late 1990s.
3 See also section "Consultation within a firm".
4 The standards also require documentation of specific risks of material misstatement due to fraud that are identified during the session (i.e. fraud ideas) and the resulting fraud risk assessment (Carpenter 2007; AICPA 2002).
5 The simple guidelines proposed by Osborn (1957) are a) criticism is ruled out; b) freewheeling is welcome, and the wilder the idea, the better; c) quantity is required; and d) combination and improvement are sought.
6 Nominal electronic brainstorming describes a technique in which members of the team input ideas individually with no interaction with the rest of the team, following which all individually generated ideas are merged and are available for the team to view (Lynch et al. 2009; Dennis and Reinicke 2004).
7 Available at https://www.ifac.org/system/files/publications/files/A%20Frame work%20for%20Audit%20Quality.pdf
8 For each document, we analyzed the last year available at the moment of writing.
9 Directive 2006/43/Ec of The European Parliament and of The Council dated May 17, 2006, states that: "Statutory auditors and audit firms that carry out statutory audit(s) of public-interest entities must publish on their websites, within three months of the end of each financial year, annual transparency reports that include at least the following: (a) a description of the legal structure and ownership; (b) where the audit firm belongs to a network, a description of the network

and the legal and structural arrangements in the network; (c) a description of the governance structure of the audit firm; (d) a description of the internal quality control system of the audit firm and a statement by the administrative or management body on the effectiveness of its functioning; (e) an indication of when the last quality assurance review referred to in Article 29 took place; (f) a list of public-interest entities for which the audit firm has carried out statutory audits during the preceding financial year; (g) a statement concerning the audit firm's independence practices which also confirms that an internal review of independence compliance has been conducted; (h) a statement on the policy followed by the audit firm concerning the continuing education of statutory auditors referred to in Article 13". Retrieved from http://eur-lex.europa.eu/legal-content/EN/TXT/PDF/?uri=CELEX:32006L0043&from=EN

10 The audit quality report is a summary report of the quality results achieved and of the planned improvements and investments in quality and technology for the future, with an additional focus on the company culture.

11 The annual review is a summary report of the performance metrics, of the company strategy, of the services provided and of the employees and their career paths.

12 Retrieved from https://assets.kpmg.com/content/dam/kpmg/pdf/2016/01/supplement-to-the-2015-kpmg-intl-transparency-report.pdf

13 Retrieved from http://www.pwc.com/gx/en/about-pwc/global-annual-review-2015/campaign-site/pwc-global-annual-review-2015.pdf

14 Retrieved from http://www.ey.com/Publication/vwLUAssets/EY_Global_review_2015/$FILE/EY_Global_review_2015.pdf

15 Retrieved from https://www2.deloitte.com/content/dam/Deloitte/us/Documents/regulatory/us-regulatory-deloitte-touche-llp-audit-quality-report-2015.pdf

References

Abdolmohammadi, M. (1999) A comprehensive taxonomy of audit task structure, professional rank and decision aids for behavioral research. *Behavioral Research in Accounting*, *11*, 51–92.

Abdolmohammadi, M., and Wright, A. (1987) An examination of the effects of experience and task complexity on audit judgments. *Accounting Review*, *62*, 1–13.

American Institute of Certified Public Accountants (AICPA). (1978) Commission on auditors' responsibilities (Cohen Commission). *Commission on Auditors' Responsibilities: Report, Conclusions and Recommendations*. New York: AICPA.

American Institute of Certified Public Accountants (AICPA). (2002) AU Section 316. *Consideration of Fraud in a Financial Statement Audit*. Retrieved from www.aicpa.org/Research/Standards/AuditAttest/DownloadableDocuments/AU-00316.pdf

Asare, S. K., and Wright, A. M. (2004) The effectiveness of alternative risk assessment and program planning tools in a fraud setting. *Contemporary Accounting Research*, *21*(2), 325–352.

Ashton, A. H. (1991) Experience and error frequency knowledge as potential determinants of audit expertise. *The Accounting Review*, *66*(2), 218–239.

Beasley, M. S., and Jenkins, J. G. (2003) A primer for brainstorming fraud risks. *Journal of Accountancy*, *196*(6), 32.

Bédard, J. C., Chi, M. T., Graham, L. E., and Shanteau, J. (1993) Expertise in auditing: Discussion. *Auditing, 12*(supplement), 21.

Bédard, J. C., and Johnstone, K. M. (2010) Audit partner tenure and audit planning and pricing. *Auditing: A Journal of Practice & Theory, 29*(2), 45–70.

Boritz, J. E., Kochetova-Kozloski, N., and Robinson, L. (2015) Are fraud specialists relatively more effective than auditors at modifying audit programs in the presence of fraud risk? *The Accounting Review, 90*(3), 881–915.

Brazel, J. F., and Agoglia, C. P. (2007) An examination of auditor planning judgments in a complex accounting information system environment. *Contemporary Accounting Research, 24*(4), 1059–1083.

Brazel, J. F., Carpenter, T. D., and Jenkins, J. G. (2010) Auditors' use of brainstorming in the consideration of fraud: Reports from the field. *The Accounting Review, 85*(4), 1273–1301.

Brody, R. G., and Moscove, S. A. (1998) Mandatory auditor rotation. *National Public Accountant, 43*, 32–35.

Carcello, J. V., and Nagy, A. L. (2004) Audit firm tenure and fraudulent financial reporting. *Auditing: A Journal of Practice & Theory, 23*(2), 55–69.

Carpenter, T. D. (2007) Audit team brainstorming, fraud risk identification, and fraud risk assessment: Implications of SAS no. 99. *The Accounting Review, 82*(5), 1119–1140.

Dennis, A. R., and Reinicke, B. A. (2004) Beta versus VHS and the acceptance of electronic brainstorming technology. *MIS Quarterly, 28*(1), 1–20.

Dereli, T., Baykasoğlu, A., and Daş, G. S. (2007) Fuzzy quality-team formation for value added auditing: A case study. Journal of Engineering and Technology Management, 24(4), 366–394.

Ellifsen, A., Knechel, W. R., and Wallage, P. (2001) Application of the business risk audit model: A field study. *Accounting Horizons, 15*(3), 193–207.

Ellifsen, A., Messier, W., Glover, S. M., and Prawitt, D. F. (2013) *Auditing and Assurance Services*. New York: McGrawHill Higher Education.

Einhorn, H. J., Hogarth, R. M., and Klempner, E. (1977) Quality of group judgment. *Psychological Bulletin, 84*(1), 158–172.

Emby, C., and Gibbins, M. (1987) Good judgment in public accounting: Quality and justification. *Contemporary Accounting Research, 4*(1), 287–313.

Farmer, T. A., Rittenberg, L. E, and Trompeter, G. M. (1987) An investigation of the impact of economic and organizational factors on auditor independence. *Auditing: A Journal of Practice and Theory, 7*(1), 1–14.

Fried, Y., Ben-David, H., Tiegs, R., Avital, N., and Yeverechyahu, U. (1998) The interactive effect of role conflict and role ambiguity on job performance. *Journal of Occupational and Organizational Psychology, 71*, 19–27.

Geiger, M. A., and Raghunandan, K. (2002) Auditor tenure and audit reporting failures. *Auditing: A Journal of Practice & Theory, 21*, 67–78.

Goetsch, D. L., and Davis, S. B. (2002) *Understanding and Implementing ISO 9000:2000*. New York: Prentice Hall.

Gold, A., Knechel, W. R., and Wallage, P. (2012) The effect of the strictness of consultation requirements on fraud consultation. *The Accounting Review, 87*(3), 925–949.

Hammersley, J. S. (2006) Pattern identification and industry-specialist auditors. *The Accounting Review, 81*(2), 309–336.

Hoffman, V. B., and Zimbelman, M. F. (2009) Do strategic reasoning and brainstorming help auditors change their standard audit procedures in response to fraud risk? *The Accounting Review, 84*(3), 811–837.

Hoyle, J. (1978) Mandatory auditor rotation: The arguments and an alternative. *Journal of Accountancy, 14*(5), 69–78.

Kadous, K., Leiby, J., and Peecher, M. E. (2013) How do auditors weight informal contrary advice? The joint influence of advisor social bond and advice justifiability. *The Accounting Review, 88*(6), 2061–2087.

Kennedy, J., Kleinmuntz, D. N., and Peecher, M. E. (1997) Determinants of the justifiability of performance in ill-structured audit tasks. *Journal of Accounting Research, 35*, 105–123.

Klein, G. (1999) *Sources of Power: How People Make Decisions*. Cambridge, MA: MIT Press.

Lindow, P. E., and Race, J. D. (2002) Beyond traditional audit techniques. *Journal of Accountancy, 194*(1), 28–33.

Livatino, M., Pecchiari N., and Pogliani, G. (2011) *Auditing: Il manuale operativo per la revisione legale dei conti*. Milan: EGEA.

Low, K. Y. (2004) The effects of industry specialization on audit risk assessments and audit-planning decisions. *The Accounting Review, 79*(1), 201–219.

Lynch, A. L., Murthy, U. S., and Engle, T. J. (2009) Fraud brainstorming using computer-mediated communication: The effects of brainstorming technique and facilitation. *The Accounting Review, 84*(4), 1209–1232.

Maister, D. H. (1982) Balancing the professional service firm. *Sloan Management Review, 24*(1), 15–29.

Mautz, R. K., and Sharaf, A. (1961) The philosophy of auditing. *Monograph No. 6*. Sarasota, FL: American Accounting Association.

McLaren, N. L. (1958) Rotation of auditors. *Journal of Accountancy, 106*(1), 41–44.

Moroney, R., and Carey, P. (2011) Industry-versus task-based experience and auditor performance. *Auditing: A Journal of Practice & Theory, 30*(2), 1–18.

Moroney, R., and Simnett, R. (2009) Differences in industry specialist knowledge and business risk identification and evaluation. *Behavioral Research in Accounting, 21*(2), 73–89.

Muczyk, J. P., Smith, E. P., and Davis, G. (1986) Holding accountants accountable: Why audits fail, how they can succeed. *Business Horizons, 29*(6), 22–28.

Myers, J. N., Myers, L. A., and Omer, T. C. (2003) Exploring the term of the auditor-client relationship and the quality of earnings: A case for mandatory auditor rotation? *The Accounting Review, 78*(3), 779–799.

Nelson, M. W., Proell, C. A., and Randel, A. (2016) Team-oriented leadership, audit risk and auditors' willingness to raise audit issues. *The Accounting Review, 91*(6), 1781–1805.

Osborn, A. F. (1957) *Applied Imagination: Principles and Procedures of Creative Thinking*, 2nd ed. New York: Charles Scribner's Sons.

Owhoso, V. E., Messier, Jr., W. F., and Lynch, Jr., J. G. (2002) Error detection by industry-specialized teams during sequential audit review. *Journal of Accounting Research, 40*(3), 883–900.

Petty, R., and Cuganesan, S. (1996) Auditor rotation: Framing the debate. *Australian Accountant, 66*(4), 40–41.

Ramsay, R. J. (1994) Senior/manager differences in audit workpaper review performance. *Journal of Accounting Research, 32*(1), 127–135.

Schultz Jr, J. J., and Reckers, P. M. (1981) The impact of group processing on selected audit disclosure decisions. *Journal of Accounting Research, 19*(2), 482–501.

Shockley, R. A. (1981) Perceptions of auditors' independence: An empirical analysis. *The Accounting Review, 56*(4), 785–800.

Solomon, I. (1987) Multi-auditor judgment/decision making research. *Journal of Accounting Literature,* 6: 1–25.

Solomon, I., Shields, M., and Whittington, R. (1999) What do industry-specialist auditors know? *Journal of Accounting Research, 37*(1), 191–208.

Taylor, M. H. (2000) The effects of industry specialization on auditors' inherent risk assessments and confidence judgements. *Contemporary Accounting Research, 17*(4), 693–712.

Trotman, K. T., Bauer, T. D., and Humphreys, K. A. (2015) Group judgment and decision making in auditing: Past and future research. *Accounting, Organizations and Society, 47*, 56–72.

Trotman, K. T., Simnett, R., and Khalifa, A. (2009) Impact of the type of audit team discussions on auditors' generation of material frauds. *Contemporary Accounting Research, 26*(4), 1115–1142.

Udeh, I. A. (2015) Audit team formation. *Journal of Legal Issues and Cases in Business, 3*, 1–6.

Vera-Muñoz, S. C., Ho, J. L., and Chow, C. W. (2006) Enhancing knowledge sharing in public accounting firms. *Accounting Horizons, 20*(2), 133–155.

Wooten, T. C. (2003) Research about audit quality. *CPA Journal, 73*(1), 48–64.

5   Auditing teams control

Introduction

The problem of organizing a team consists of achieving cooperation among a set of individuals who share only to a certain extent congruent objectives. Ouchi (1979) presented a framework that distinguishes between three forms of control that can be used to maintain and expand the convergence of these objectives: output, behaviour and ceremonial forms of control, which can be implemented respectively by means of the efficient operation of a market, the rules of a bureaucracy and the social agreements incorporated in a clan. These forms of control are characterized by some general social and informational dimensions.

The social dimensions refer to the set of agreements between the individuals of a team. A market is based on a norm of reciprocity. This norm ensures that if one individual cheats, he or she is sanctioned by all the other individuals of the team in which he or she is incorporated. The cost of this norm is related to the fact that it is necessary to guarantee that the parties of the social system behave honestly. If this cannot be assumed then each party must introduce suitable monitoring mechanisms such as surveillance means, complete contracting and enforcement, in order to avoid opportunistic behaviours (Williamson 1975). A bureaucracy is based not only on a norm of reciprocity, but also on an arrangement on a legitimate authority. This latter is hierarchically superior to the other members of the team and has the right to command and monitor lower individuals. Finally, a clan is characterized by not only a norm of reciprocity and the presence of a legitimate authority, but also by the achievement of a social agreement on a broad range of values and beliefs. This is based on a shared understanding of what represents proper behaviour, and on a substantial commitment on the part of each individual to these socially defined behaviours (Ouchi 1979).

The informational dimensions refer to the set of symbols with which the individuals of a team communicate complex ideas. In a market context, the information necessary to operate an output mode of control is incorporated in internal indicators of output, which serve the function of prices. In a bureaucratic environment, the information is contained in an explicit set of rules related to both expected behaviours and levels of output. In this case, though it is never possible to specify the rules that cover every single contingency, the information problem can be addressed by covering the majority of contingent events and by leaving the remaining possibilities to the legitimate authority. In a clan the information is contained in the rituals, stories and ceremonies, which express the values and beliefs of the organization (Ouchi 1979).

Apart from the previously mentioned social and informational dimensions, the various forms of control are suitable in specific contexts. In particular, when there is a high ability to measure output or a high knowledge of the transformation process, the formal output and behaviour controls tend to be effective. On the contrary, Ouchi (1979) argued that when these conditions are absent the more subtle form of clan control is required.

In an auditing environment, first, market levers play a key role in defining the overall targets for cost and quality control procedures. These relate to the general level of demand for audit services, their regulatory framework, competition and fee pressure, and the supply of good calibre audit staff. Market controls and the related indicators used in terms of both quality and cost dimensions are pervasive and affect staff at all the levels of the organization's hierarchy. The impact of market levers on cost control can be found in the analysis of variances between time records and time budget, with a specific focus on budget overruns. The effect of market levers on audit quality is more diverse and refers to professional standards, legal requirements, and risk of litigation. Second, bureaucratic controls are used extensively and refer to the formal review of audit working papers, compliance with the firm's audit methodology and supervision of junior staff. Finally, clan controls are important mechanisms to achieve an appropriate balance between trust relationships and mentoring (Otley and Pierce 1996a; Sweeney and Pierce 2004; Pierce and Sweeney 2005, 2006; Jeppesen 2007; McGarry and Sweeney 2007).

Auditing teams and the review process

One of the most important bureaucratic controls in auditing firms is represented by the review process, which consists of members of the audit team evaluating the activities carried out by other members. Normally this process takes place in a hierarchical and sequential fashion. Gradually reviews are conducted, while the process moves up from the base of the team to the partners. They are meant to ensure that the opinion given is appropriate and the necessary documentation has been prepared. In this way, the judgements are of better quality because an additional person has been added at each step, with a corresponding beneficial diversification effect. The quality is, moreover, enhanced by the interaction effect deriving from the discussion between the members that have carried out the work and the reviewer, and the hierarchical effect, resulting from the intervention of a professional of a higher rank who selects the relative weights for the different inputs to the judgement (Libby and Trotman 1993; Rich, Solomon, and Trotman 1997; Trotman, Bauer, and Humphreys 2015).

Thanks to the review process, audit effectiveness improves because both conceptual and mechanical errors are identified by different professional roles in the team (Ramsay 1994; Harding and Trotman 1999).

The review process can be conducted in many different ways. Normally, the work papers are analyzed by the reviewers, and review notes are written for the preparer and sent electronically for a response or discussed face-to-face in real-time interacting reviews. Reviews can be either all-encompassing or specialized. Evidence shows that the first types of reviews are substantially more accurate than the second and that they require less time for seniors and managers to conduct (Ismail and Trotman 1995; Bamber and Ramsay 2000).

The review process is articulated in different phases: planning, message acquisition, elaboration, evaluation and decision/action selection, as described by Rich et al. (1997).

- *Planning.* At this stage the reviewer collects information and trades-off the different positive and negative elements of the various courses of action. These actions relate to the extent and type of review activities and are related to environmental factors such as the perception of the client (e.g. control risk and integrity of personnel) and the preparer (e.g. competence and incentives). Environmental information is normally retrieved from memory and integrated with additional elements coming from reading the audit program, the planning memo and preparers notes, and discussions with other audit team members or even analytical procedures. In addition, during the review task, new information may emerge that requires the reviewer to update his or her perception of preparers competence.
- *Message acquisition.* During this phase, the reviewer gathers information about the preparer's performance of assigned audit procedures. This information is collected from the working papers and directly from the preparer. This message acquisition may be changed during the review process due to the perceived costs and benefits of the different activities to carry out. For example, if there are budget constraints and

time is a scarce resource, the reviewer may decide not to acquire the preparer's messages linked to low-risk areas and focus attention closely and read the working papers and discuss with the preparer the higher-risk areas.

- *Elaboration.* At this point, the reviewer analyzes all the information collected in order to evaluate the appropriateness of the preparer's activities. To do so different tasks are carried out: internally, re-computation of calculations employed by the preparer, logic verification according to previous experience and knowledge of the client, counterfactual reasoning, and so on; externally, reference to professional opinions, interaction with other members of the firm, request of additional information to the preparer, and so on. Moreover, other information may be pertinent at his stage to identify potential alternative explanations of financial-statements values and trends that could not be explained with the information provided by the preparer.
- *Decision/action selection.* In this final process, all the information collected in the previous steps is combined and used to for developing a judgement on the preparer work and on potential errors in the information provided. The analysis of the information can lead to one of the following responses: (1) acceptance of the preparer's work, (2) collection of additional evidence to be analyzed, (3) request of explanation of the work done, (4) gathering of new documents, or (5) a combination of the previous actions. Depending on the decision taken, the reviewer writes or reports the necessary steps the preparer has to follow to comply with the concerns of the reviewer. In turn, the preparer addresses these concerns and resubmits the working papers to the reviewer, who assesses the related revision. This cycle continues until the reviewer provides acceptance of the working papers, which are passed to the reviewer's superior for further review, if necessary (Rich et al. 1997).

The review process seems to be affected by two categories of variables: environmental factors and reviewer-specific characteristics (Rich et al. 1997; Trotman et al. 2015). In relation to the effects of environmental factors, there are the conditions, circumstances and influences surrounding the review task and relate to information presentation structures, the planning memorandum, time pressure, aggressive financial reporting, the task and complexity of the setting, and audit risk and information importance (Rich, Solomon, and Trotman 1997; Trotman et al. 2015). For example, higher levels of audit risk lead to more accuracy of evidence recall and attention to aggressive financial statement reporting (Sprinkle and Tubbs 1998; Phillips 1999; Trotman et al. 2015). With reference to reviewer-specific characteristics, each reviewer is characterized by different competencies (e.g.

procedural and declarative), different personal features and preferences (e.g. tolerance for risk and ambiguity), a certain memory structure, and more generally a specific combination of individual-specific characteristics. For example, Asare and McDaniel (1996) found that reviewers do their work more times when it is completed by an unknown preparer than when the preparer is familiar and that the familiarity with the preparer and the task complexity interact to determine the ability of the reviewer in detecting conclusion errors. Tan and Jamal (2001) investigated whether the reviewers' evaluation of the quality of preparers' work is affected by the opinion they have about the preparers and found that average managers evaluate more positively memos developed by outstanding seniors than memos written by average seniors, once they know the identity of the preparer, but outstanding managers are not subject to the same effect.

One important novelty related to the review process, and more in general to the other bureaucratic controls, is that recently there has been an increasing move from a diagnostic use of these controls, where the focus was on compliance with pre-specified procedures and attention directed to any exceptional audit findings, to an interactive form. This means that the audit review process has changed from being primarily a review of audit files in the absence of the audit team to a "review by interview". This involves the partner and manager analyzing the working papers on site and in the presence of the audit team members and discussing the audit work with them. This change results in a high level of interaction with, and questioning of, the audit team. Partners are personally involved in decisions taken prior to the beginning of the audit regarding the scope of the audit testing, and following the completion of the fieldwork concerning the suitability of the work completed to produce the final audit opinion (Pierce and Sweeney 2005). Pierce and Sweeney (2005) provided evidence of this change by means of semi-structured interviews with partners from three of the Big 4 firms. Their findings show that the audit review process represents the most important control mechanism over the quality of the auditing work and that it has changed from being primarily a review of audit files to a "review by interview" where partner and managers review the working papers and discuss with all the members of the audit team. More attention is concentrated on the risky areas, and probing questions are asked to test whether the staff and seniors understand the process. This change is accompanied by a corresponding reduction in the level of documentation. It results in a higher number of visits to the job by the partner and the manager before the auditors are leaving the site to avoid the need of revisiting. This continuous monitoring implies an ability to review almost on real time, checking in each moment what the members of the team are doing, an aspect that is particularly important when deadlines are particularly tight. In addition, it allows to identify quality threatening behaviours and to prevent them, given that auditors are aware of the review process. Finally, evidence suggests that audit partners have different styles in the audit review. Some pay a lot of attention to the details uniformly, whereas some others adapt their style depending on the risk factors related to a job, including time pressure. In general, they tend to avoid re-performing the work, because it is perceived contrary to the core values of integrity and trust (Pierce and Sweeney 2005).

Audit methodology

The audit methodology has undergone a process of transformation in recent times, as reported in a study by Pierce and Sweeney (2005). The auditing activities are carried out by a team on the basis of a structured process, with the majority of the documents developed and stored in electronic format. Compliance with the methodology represents the basis for the quality control approach. According to Pierce and Sweeney (2005) the audit methodology has gradually incorporated more involvement of partners and managers both before and during the audit process in ascertaining the risks and in understanding the client's business and control system. This new approach is thus focused on identifying high-risk business areas and concentrating the work on those areas, with the support of specific audit software. The activities of the junior auditors have become more customized to the specific clients' needs and not on the standard work programmes, and less risky areas are assigned to more junior staff. In addition, briefing meetings are an essential part of the methodology to make sure that the staff fully understands the client and how to address the related risks.

Auditing teams and clan control

Clan controls are particularly applicable in an audit environment, as the conditions necessary to adopt them are often present (Macintosh 1985). In a clan, individuals think that their specific interests can be met by means of a strong embeddedness in the interests of the team and of the entire organization to which they belong (Macintosh 1985). They are so strongly socialized in the context that their interests tend to overlap with that of the clan and they make decisions that support the objectives of the organization (Ouchi 1980; Ouchi and Price 1993). Because of this reason, clan control requires stability of membership and a strong social memory (Ouchi 1984). However, given that it is not possible to achieve a perfect fit between the people and the organization in which they are incorporated, performance evaluation mechanisms play an important role. In a clan environment, they cannot be translated into explicit, verifiable performance measures and tend to be informal and based on a subtle reading of signals (Ouchi 1980; Pierce and Sweeney 2005).

McGarry and Sweeney (2007) suggest that clan controls are based on specific distinctive elements that require the existence of certain pre-conditions to be implemented successfully (Macintosh 1985). These are: partner intuition, informal communication, image management and selection and training procedures.

Partner intuition

The intuition of partners and their "sixth sense" are considered important elements of clan control because they are the way in which more senior auditors put their experience and insight in operation. There are certain informal procedures that are activated through the instinct and intuition of the partners and represent relevant means of the control system. These elements are important for issues such as knowing what questions to ask during the review by interview and knowing which audits require additional review time. The intuition of partners is vitally key also in deciding when the partner needs to implement additional monitoring as necessary or when the development of trust is more appropriate. In particular, when the commitment to the objectives of the team are less strong or there is a conflict between the team's objectives and the individual objectives, then the partner's intuition and judgement represent important levers to define a suitable balance between trust and compatible modes of control. In addition, general intuition is at the basis of information transmitted through the partners' information communication network concerning evaluation of individual auditors' performance and the selection of the best quality recruits, given that when they reach the final steps of the selection process they all possess the necessary qualifications (Pierce and Sweeney 2005; McGarry and Sweeney 2007).

Informal communication

Informal communication takes place regularly by means of networks activated between partners, managers, and individual junior auditors on issues related to performance, which may be difficult to incorporate in formal performance evaluation processes. In particular, the informal communication activated by partners and managers is important to select staff for job bookings and for identifying team members that need a stronger control, thus reducing the risk of inaccurate or unfair assessments. Moreover, in a context of relevant time pressures the communication of the performance evaluation information to the staff members is conducted on an informal basis and allows them to focus on the efforts that auditors put in their activities. Informal communication is seen as particularly effective especially when there is a suspicion that auditors minimize effort without sufficient evidence to prove this type of behaviour. Finally, this form of communication is useful to link certain auditors to specific type of audits, with weaker auditors involved in small client audits or to no audit in case of surplus capacity and high-rated auditors included in teams dedicated to bigger and more high-profile engagements where there are more possibilities to interact with audit managers and partners and learn from them. One disadvantage that may derive from these dynamics is that auditors focus too much on points that are of particular interest to partners, leading to inadequate attention given to some other issues of an audit (Pierce and Sweeney 2005; McGarry and Sweeney 2007).

Image management

Auditing firms are particularly image conscious and try to make sure that they are presenting a positive image of their control of audit quality both within the organization and also externally to the public and clients (McGarry and Sweeney 2007). This image is protected by leveraging on formal controls for audit opinions. These formal controls are, in fact, seen as easier to use as a defence in case of litigation than the pure informal procedures and partners' intuition and assume priority in promoting the external image of the firm. Furthermore, evidence shows that the image is protected by refusing to question the integrity of auditors or to re-perform the work. In fact, while there is indication of the existence of quality-threatening behaviours in auditing firms, often there is no open discussion and explicit recognition of the risk of these behaviours so that there is no need to address this risk. There is not even evidence in empirical studies that this issue is included in staff-training processes, that there are procedures to face alleged cases of auditors taking these behaviours, or that there are sanctions applied to those individuals that are found responsible for wrongdoing (Pierce and Sweeney 2005).

Selection and training procedures

Recruiting people that are suitable to become auditors is a key dimension of clan control, and partners are normally directly involved in these selection processes. Yet, in practice, the perfect match between the person and the job is hardly achieved and therefore training procedures contribute to filling the voids of the recruiting process. These training procedures may take different forms: as formal courses, "on the job" training, "peer" training and "in the corridor" training. Additionally, mentoring is another important element of clan control, which sustains career development, social support and role modelling. This latter takes place mainly with a passive socialization process, whereby protégés learn by observing the mentor, in an informal fashion (Scandura and Viator 1994). Finally, integrity and professionalisms of individual auditors are further aspects of selection and training procedures because they represent safeguards against quality-threatening behaviours by making sure that auditors do not activate any quality-compromising action due to their strong sense of commitment to their own professional values and concern for the current and future states of the profession (Pierce and Sweeney 2005; McGarry and Sweeney 2007).

Quality-threatening behaviours by auditors

Existing contributions in the literature have provided evidence of the existence of dysfunctional behaviours undertaken by auditors in performing their activities (Pierce and Sweeney 2004, 2006; Sweeney and Pierce 2004; Peytcheva and Gillet 2012; Johansen and Christoffersen 2016). The most reported ones can be related to three different areas: premature sign off (PMSO), under-reporting of timing (URT) and audit quality reduction behaviour (AQRB) (Otley and Pierce 1996a).

Premature sign off

This behaviour is related to the fact that an auditor signs off a required audit step without completing a specific activity, which is not addressed in another audit phase, without noting the omission. The implications deriving from this behaviour are particularly severe because they have an implication in terms of the contents of the audit opinion (Otley and Pierce 1996a).

Under-reporting of time

This behaviour is linked to the fact that an auditor carries out the activities and uses extra time which is not charged to the client for whom the work was carried out. Even if this behaviour per se does not have immediate implications on auditing quality in the short run, it may have an impact in the long run. In fact, given that the previous year's recorded time represents a reference point for planning the following years' budgets, under-reporting of time may lead to tight time budgets in the future and this in turn may have consequences on the quality of the work done (Otley and Pierce 1996a). Sweeney and Pierce (2006) suggested that under-reporting of time is an umbrella term that includes a set of behaviours with different and distinct motivational influences. Although these behaviours seem to have the same effect in terms of charging less time to a specific client than the amount of hours spent for that client, the drivers of these behaviours and the corresponding consequences for the individual auditor, the firm and the profession differ substantially, as well as the related perspectives of audit partners and seniors. There are six types of behaviours that can be attributed to under-reporting of timing.

- *Voluntary time adjustment.* This is the least harmful behaviour and arises when an individual auditor considers that part of the time spent for the client is not in line with efficiency standards and therefore should not be charged to the client. The reason for this consideration may be related to the perceived personal level of efficiency and personal judgement of what constitutes a "good" hour and should be charged to the client, without receiving any input from a superior. This type of behaviour is not in fact a real under-reporting of time, but simply a behaviour that compensates the lower level of productivity, which should not in fact be charged to the client. This type of behaviour has many positive implications related to facilitating an adjustment for inefficiencies that the auditor attributes to personal performance and allows the auditor to assess the time that should be charged to the client. In addition, this type of behaviour may contribute to the learning and development of individual auditors by providing the motivation to identify and react to inefficient work activities and thus increase the future level of performance (Sweeney and Pierce 2006).
- *Voluntary unrecorded time.* This behaviour refers to the case in which the auditor voluntarily reduces time charged to the client because of perceived personal inefficiency, but this lack of efficiency could be related to causes that do not depend on the individual auditor, such as lack of experience or insufficient training. The time that is not charged to the client should be recorded as in an account including all the non-chargeable costs, but it normally remains at the expense of the individual auditor, who feels a personal responsibility for the lack of experience and feels that peers are operating at a higher level of efficiency. This behaviour seems to have positive consequences related to the fact that individual auditors report a good performance in comparison to their more experienced peers, the level of performance increases in terms of chargeable hours out of the total hours supplied, and the client is charged only for productive time. However, this behaviour can activate dangerous defence mechanisms that may damage the company (Sweeney and Pierce 2006).
- *Pressurized time adjustment and pressurized unrecorded time.* These types of behaviors refer to reducing the time actually recorded for a

specific client, despite the time worked is considered as productive and efficient and without any specific intervention by superiors. In this situation, the behaviour is undertaken because of an external pressure to meet certain budget targets as an important aspect to achieving a good performance evaluation. This kind of behaviour seems to have immediate positive consequences: the auditor avoids the risk of developing a bad reputation and superiors avoid fee recovery difficulties and potentially problematic fee renegotiations with the client. However, in the long run, in case of reallocation of non-chargeable time to a specific account, this leads to what is called pressurized time adjustments, which have the potential to demotivate auditors due to the understatement of chargeable hours and related devaluation of the work carried out by the auditor. When this reallocation is not possible, auditors feel the pressure to avoid recording the extra time in their timesheets, leading to what is called pressurized unrecorded time (Sweeney and Pierce 2006).

• *Instructed time adjustment and instructed unrecorded time.* These types of behaviours differ from the previous categories because they are triggered by a superior, normally a manager, and are implemented by a senior who feels he or she has to follow the indications of the superior. The superior is motivated to initiate such behaviour because he or she fears fee recovery difficulties which could damage her or his reputation and impair client relationships. When the instruction is to simply reallocate time to an account of non-chargeable time, a behaviour called instructed time adjustment, the implications on the senior seem to be rather limited. However, when the instruction from the superior is not to record the time completely with the corresponding effects in terms of loss of associated pay, the consequences on the senior are more relevant and relate to loss of motivation, high turnover and performing fewer audit procedures. These types of behaviours are more serious in that they imply breaching the official firm policies to achieve short-term objectives (Sweeney and Pierce 2006).

Audit quality reduction behaviour in general

These behaviours refer to a general umbrella of actions that threaten auditing quality, such as for example accepting a limited amount of explanation for an issue that was submitted to the client, revising the documents only superficially and so on (Otley and Pierce 1996a).

Pierce and Sweeney (2004) did an empirical analysis of the quality-threatening behaviours and found that 43 per cent of auditors reported acceptance of limited client explanations and superficial analysis of client documents. They also found that other quality-threatening behaviours were less frequent, such as biasing of sample selection in favour of less problematic items (36 per cent), reliance on client work more than appropriate (31 per cent), failure to research an accounting principle (29 per cent), premature sign off (24 per cent) and reduction of work on an audit step below what is considered valid (21 per cent).

Determinants of quality-threatening behaviours by auditors

Many of the organizational factors that can have an effect on quality-threatening behaviours were started to be studied in the 1980s (Alderman and Deitrick 1982; Kelley and Margheim 1987). During the 1990s little attention was dedicated to these aspects and a renewed focus was activated in the 2000s when new contributors analyzed the variables and the relationships with quality-threatening behaviours. The main variables are set out in the following sections (Pierce and Sweeney 2004, 2006; Sweeney and Pierce 2004; Peytcheva and Gillet 2012).

Time pressure

Extant contributions have defined time pressure as time budget pressure. In turn, budget pressure has been studied in the management accounting literature as budget tightness and specificity of budget targets. It has also been investigated in the audit firms' literature as budget attainability (Pierce and Sweeney 2004). With reference to budget tightness, there is conflicting evidence concerning the relationship with quality threatening behaviours (Sweeney and Pierce 2004). Kelley and Margheim (1990) found an inverted U-shaped relationship between budget tightness and quality-threatening behaviour, suggesting that up to a certain point budget tightness is positively associated with quality-threatening behaviours, but that beyond a specific level this relationship becomes negative. Other contributions have found that this relationship remains positive and does not decline (Otley and Pierce 1996b; Pierce and Sweeney 2004). An alternative-opposite, but overlapping, variable that was taken into consideration was related to budget attainability, and was found to be negatively related to quality-threatening behaviours (Otley and Pierce 1996a; Pierce and Sweeney 2004). Some other contributors have equated time pressure with time deadline pressure, intended as adequacy of time booking to job, pressure to work on another assignment and client imposed deadline (DeZoort and Lord 1997; Pierce and Sweeney 2004). Sweeney and Pierce (2004) conducted a more fine-grained, in-depth qualitative investigation of the previously mentioned variables and explained both the different types of time pressure and the related perceived causes. Time pressure can result from one or a combination of external time deadlines, internal time deadlines and time budgets, and was found to be increasing over time. The main distinction was found to be between the pressure to have the work completed within a certain deadline (deadline pressure) and the pressure to control the amount of hours charged to a job (budget pressure). The key variables that explain time pressure in general, and more specifically internal deadlines, were related to the imbalance between the supply and demand of staff and audits given that the additional audit work was not sufficiently matched with the additional staffing. Resources were perceived to be stretched to the limit given that all the auditors have very strict deadlines to complete their activities. Another variable was related to the pressure activated by clients, who impose audit fee reductions, define unrealistic time deadlines, propose changes in timing of the audit work and are characterized by a lack of preparation. A further aspect was connected to the new risk-based audit approach and a related emphasis on cost reduction. Finally, other variables that have an impact on time pressure are audit-specific influences, pressures from international auditors, the volume of technical material, the bargaining power of the manager in getting staff for the job, the employee grading system where auditors from the same intake can have different charge-out rates depending on their educational background and the amount of time spent by the manager on review. Sweeney and Pierce (2004) investigated also in detail a range of negative impacts of time pressure. They found that there is not a general consensus on what should be considered as a desirable degree of time pressure and that most of the auditors interviewed found that the existing level of time pressure was far higher than desirable, with personal consequences in terms of reduced morale and motivation, increased health problems, tiredness and overall lower standard of life and higher turnover. In general, there was a perception that more time pressure activated dysfunctional responses in terms of biasing sample selection, greater than appropriate reliance on client work, decreased scepticism, phantom ticking and an overall lower standard of work. Other negative implications of high time pressure were perceived to be linked to a lower level of training, increased responsibility and reduced levels of supervision, with potential activation of inadvertent quality-threatening behaviours.

Budgetary participation

Participation in target setting is another variable that has been indicated as potentially impacting the level of quality-threatening behaviours. However, conflicting results have been reported on the relationship between these two variables (Pierce and Sweeney 2004; Sweeney and Pierce 2004). In their qualitative examination of the management control in audit firms, Sweeney and Pierce (2004) found that both internal and external deadlines were considered to be impossible to be affected by seniors and that the conditions that are normally indicated as relevant for participation – in particular the information asymmetry between the manager and the senior – are rarely occurring in auditing firms. This information asymmetry, in fact, occurs only in particular circumstances, like the case in which the senior auditor has worked in the same audit in previous years. In addition, even if seniors are involved in planning, it may be for jobs that they would not work for, and the involvement takes place simply because they are available at the time of planning, and in any case they have no real influence on setting targets. Moreover, this may result in a disadvantage to the senior given that she or he has no knowledge of the accuracy of the time charged in the previous year and the audit environment is characterized by a level of uncertainty related to the amount of time needed for a specific job that the senior would not be in a position to reduce. In conclusion, Sweeney and Pierce (2004) suggest that the characteristics of the audit environment (rotating audit teams, high staff turnover and nature of audit work) make the possibility to participate in target setting very limited and generally perceived as being low. Finally, they argue that participation represents a moderating variable in the association between time pressure and quality threatening behaviours because it can lead to more motivation to meet the time target, which can have either a positive or a negative effect on behaviour. In fact, by asking seniors to participate in setting budgets, managers induce seniors to take more responsibility for the budget, with potential effects if the budgets are not met in terms of activating quality-threatening behaviours.

Style in performance evaluation

The performance of each auditor is evaluated periodically by the auditor's direct superior in the firm, and this process is of critical importance for career advancement (Kelley and Seiler 1982; Hanlon 1994). Auditors are evaluated on the bases of different aspects such as the ability to complete the audits within the specified budget and deadline, technical ability and professionalism. Furthermore, the promotion of hierarchical levels above seniors depends also on commercial skills, including the capacity to control budget. Because of these reasons, a budget-oriented style of evaluation may be linked to quality-threatening behaviours. In particular, it has been found that reliance on accounting criteria leads to under-reporting of timing, whereas a non-accounting style of evaluation leads to other quality-threatening behaviours (Pierce and Sweeney 2004).[1] In their analysis of semi-structured interviews with auditors, Sweeney and Pierce (2004) found that with the flattening of hierarchical reporting structures, juniors have started to report to managers rather than seniors, and seniors to partners instead of managers. Due to this trend, juniors may start to use their own style of operating and they are not always aware of the standards required to do the work, so that the lack of explanations of seniors may result in inadvertent quality-threatening behaviours. In addition, the authors found that in periods when there is understaffing, promotion is almost inevitable in the firm and therefore the formal performance evaluation may not have a relevant effect on individual behaviours, which would be less attentive to quality implications. Another aspect that was identified was related to the fact that the style of evaluation has changed from a budget-constrained logic to a target-constrained one, which includes emphasis on both budgets and deadlines. This is because the client does not immediately understand the quality of the work unless something relevant occurs, but will always easily notice if a deadline is missed. Therefore, the majority of respondents perceived that meeting time budgets has decreased in importance, whereas meeting the deadlines has correspondingly increased. This new style of evaluation is perceived as potentially increasing the likelihood of dysfunctional behaviour due to the reluctance of audit staff to inform managers of any problems that may have an impact on meeting the deadlines.

Consequences of quality-threatening behaviours by auditors

Quality-threatening behaviours are expected to generate important adverse effects on the output of audit firms in terms of reduced audit quality, damaged reputation and increased risk of litigation. From an individual auditor point of view, they can be interpreted as attempts to deal with pressures and tensions that are considered to be not discussable with the higher levels of the hierarchy and then generate an enhanced degree of stress and tension, with obvious consequences on employees' satisfaction and general morale (McNair 1991; Pierce and Sweeney 2006). Only few contributions, however, analyzed the effects of quality-threatening behaviours. One exception is represented by Pierce and Sweeney (2005) who investigated the negative effects of quality-threatening behaviours from the perspective of partners. They found that all the partners interviewed acknowledged the potential of these behaviours to occur and recalled specific examples of them, indicating that they could be referred to the limitations of the formal controls. In addition, they reported that high levels of pressure to meet the deadlines, rapid promotion of staff, and the more "laissez faire" approach for recent recruits due to the tough job market could be explained with the lack of competencies and motivation, which were associated with control problems and concerns about deterioration of auditing quality. Other more defensive explanations of quality-threatening behaviours that emerged during the interviews were provided with the consideration that these behaviours occurred only in non-critical audit steps, or that even if reported they were not in fact taking place, because other professionals in the firm were managing these issues and, finally, that they were simply overstated by the respondents. Seen in this way, these behaviours do not seem to generate any threat to auditing quality and do not represent a specific risk for the firm. With reference to the consequences of quality-threatening behaviours for individual auditors, Pierce and Sweeney (2005) reported that if the behaviour was not identified within the firm, the perception was that there was no consequence for the individual auditor, and in any case the likelihood of detection was low. If undetected, auditors experience mental anguish arising from the fear of detection or the auditor's ethical stance. However, the perceived low risk of detection and the explanations provided by auditors such as time pressure, lack of importance of the work and proximity to the weekend reduce this anguish (Pierce and Sweeney 2006). Even in case of detection, many partners thought that the issue should have been managed through a combination of retraining and mentoring, with only a minority of partners considering the termination of employment as an appropriate reaction. Other consequences for the individual auditor could be related to the failure to be involved in more interesting assignments in the future, poor performance evaluation and a lower rate of pay (Pierce and Sweeney 2005). In relation to the consequences for the audit firm, it was reported that when certain tests are considered critical for the quality of the work, they would probably be performed properly, indicating that auditors would be less likely to engage in quality-threatening behaviours in important areas (Pierce and Sweeney 2005). When the behaviours are not detected, the only perceived consequences were related to higher staff turnover due to low morale and perceived pressure to engage in these behaviours, the possibility of longer-term effects due to enhanced level of substandard work, and auditors maintaining a gripe against the company after they leave. Many partners were conscious that if the behaviour was detected externally they would bear the risk of litigation. If that happens, possible consequences for the audit firm refer to a reprimand from the international firm, an impact on client expectations of the rigour of the audit, a loss of firm reputation, a risk of litigation and decrease in audit fees. However, partners would envisage few consequences arising from isolated cases in less risky areas (Pierce and Sweeney 2005, 2006). For the accounting profession, the negative effects of quality-threatening behaviours were related to the adverse impact on the image of accountancy and the reduced probability of the continuation of self-regulation deriving from the detected behaviours. For the business world, the lack of detection of these behaviours and of addressing the weaknesses in clients' internal control systems due to a false sense of security by clients decreased client cooperation with auditors and led to the continuation of quality-threatening behaviours throughout an individual's career (Pierce and Sweeney 2006).

Note

1 In their work Pierce and Sweeney (2004) include in this category: acceptance of weak client explanations, superficial reviews of client documents, biasing of sample selection in favour of less troublesome items, greater than appropriate reliance of client work, failure to research an accounting principle, premature sign off, reduction in the amount of work on an audit step below what was considered reasonable, failure to complete procedures required in an audit programme step in ways other than those listed, reduction in the sample size specified in the audit programme without noting the reduction, reduction in the amount of documentation below that considered acceptable by the firm.

References

Alderman, C. W., and Deitrick, J. W. (1982) Auditors' perceptions of time budget pressures and premature sign-offs: A replication and extension. *Auditing: A Journal of Practice & Theory, 1*(2), 54–68.

Asare, S. K., and McDaniel, L. S. (1996) The effects of familiarity with the preparer and task complexity on the effectiveness of the audit review process. *The Accounting Review, 71*(2), 139–159.

Bamber, E. M., and Ramsay, R. J. (2000) The effects of specialization in audit workpaper review on review efficiency and reviewers' confidence. *Auditing: A Journal of Practice & Theory, 19*(2), 147–157.

De Zoort, F. T., and Lord, A. T. (1997) A review and synthesis of pressure effects research in accounting. *Journal of Accounting Literature, 16*, 28–86.

Harding, N., and Trotman, K. T. (1999) Hierarchical differences in audit workpaper review performance. *Contemporary Accounting Research, 16*(4), 671–684.

Ismail, Z., and Trotman, K. T. (1995) The impact of the review process in hypothesis generation tasks. *Accounting, Organizations and Society, 20*(5), 345–357.

Jeppesen, K. K. (2007) Organizational risk in large audit firms. *Managerial Auditing Journal, 22*(6), 590–603.

Johansen, T. R., and Christoffersen, J. (2016) Performance evaluations in audit firms: Evaluation foci and dysfunctional behaviour. *International Journal of Auditing*.

Kelley, T., and Margheim, L. (1987) The effect of audit billing arrangement on underreporting of time and audit quality reduction acts. *Advances in Accounting, 5*(4), 22–33.

Kelley, T., and Margheim, L. (1990) The impact of time budget pressure, personality, and leadership variables on dysfunctional auditor behavior. *Auditing: A Journal of Practice & Theory, 9*(2), 21–42.

Kelley, T., and Seller, S. E. (1982) Auditor stress and time budgets. *The CPA Journal, 52*(12), 24–34.

Libby, R., and Trotman, K. T. (1993) The review process as a control for differential recall of evidence in auditor judgments. *Accounting, Organizations and Society, 18*(6), 559–574.

Macintosh, N. B. (1985) *Social Software of Accounting and Information Systems.* Hoboken, NJ: John Wiley & Sons, Inc.

McGarry, C., and Sweeney, B. (2007) Clan type controls over audit quality – audit seniors' perspectives. *Irish Accounting Review, 14*(2), 37–59.

McNair, C. J. (1991) Proper compromises: The management control dilemma in public accounting and its impact on auditor behavior. *Accounting, Organizations and Society, 16*(7), 635–653.

Otley, D. T., and Pierce, B. J. (1996a) The operation of control systems in large audit firms. *Auditing: A Journal of Practice & Theory, 15*(2), 65–84.

Otley, D. T., and Pierce, B. J. (1996b) Auditor time budget pressure: Consequences and antecedents. *Accounting, Auditing & Accountability Journal, 9*(1), 31–58.

Ouchi, W. G. (1979) A conceptual framework for the design of organizational control mechanisms. *Management Science, 25*(9), 833–848.

Ouchi, W. G. (1980) Markets, bureaucracies, and clans. *Administrative Science Quarterly, 25*(1), 129–141.

Ouchi, W. G. (1984) The m-form society: Lessons from business management. *Human Resource Management, 23*(2), 191–213.

Ouchi, W. G., and Price, R. L. (1993) Hierarchies, clans, and theory Z: A new perspective on organization development. *Organizational Dynamics, 21*(4), 62–70.

Peytcheva, M., and Gillett, P. R. (2012) Auditor perceptions of prior involvement and reputation threats as antecedents of quality threatening audit behavior. *Managerial Auditing Journal, 27*(9), 796–820.

Phillips, F. (1999) Auditor attention to and judgments of aggressive financial reporting. *Journal of Accounting Research, 37*(1), 167–189.

Pierce, B., and Sweeney, B. (2004) Cost – quality conflict in audit firms: An empirical investigation. *European Accounting Review, 13*(3), 415–441.

Pierce, B., and Sweeney, B. (2005) Management control in audit firms – partners' perspectives. *Management Accounting Research, 16*(3), 340–370.

Pierce, B., and Sweeney, B. (2006) Perceived adverse consequences of quality threatening behaviour in audit firms. *International Journal of Auditing, 10*(1), 19–39.

Ramsay, R. J. (1994) Senior/manager differences in audit workpaper review performance. *Journal of Accounting Research, 32*(1), 127–135.

Rich, J. S., Solomon, I., and Trotman, K. T. (1997) Multi-auditor judgment/decision making research: A decade later. *Journal of Accounting Literature, 16,* 86.

Scandura, T. A., and Viator, R. E. (1994) Mentoring in public accounting firms: An analysis of mentor-protégé relationships, mentorship functions, and protégé turnover intentions. *Accounting, Organizations and Society, 19*(8), 717–734.

Sprinkle, G. B., and Tubbs, R. M. (1998) The effects of audit risk and information importance on auditor memory during working paper review. *The Accounting Review, 73*(4), 475–502.

Sweeney, B., and Pierce, B. (2004) Management control in audit firms: A qualitative examination. *Accounting, Auditing & Accountability Journal, 17*(5), 779–812.

Sweeney, B., and Pierce, B. (2006) Good hours, bad hours and auditors' defence mechanisms in audit firms. *Accounting, Auditing & Accountability Journal, 19*(6), 858–892.

Tan, H. T., and Jamal, K. (2001) Do auditors objectively evaluate their subordinates' work? *The Accounting Review, 76*(1), 99–110.

Trotman, K. T., Bauer, T. D., and Humphreys, K. A. (2015) Group judgment and decision making in auditing: Past and future research. *Accounting, Organizations and Society, 47*, 56–72.

Williamson, O. E. (1975) *Markets and Hierarchies*. New York: Free Press, 26–30.

6　Evidence from the field

Introduction

The objective of this chapter is to show insights from the practice. In particular, we report the findings collected from the field and we interpret them through the lenses of the concepts and references sketched in previous chapters. Our approach has been to compare the experience of professionals with the knowledge emerging from the literature and show whether existing conclusions are confirmed, equally emphasized or need to be revised and complemented. The focus has been, in particular, in pointing out those potential aspects and phenomena related to the functioning of the audit teams that have not been indicated in the existing research.

Research method

Our empirical work used a qualitative approach. Semi-structured interviews were conducted to collect our data over a period of eight months. Face-to-face interviews lasted about one hour. Most of them took place with two researchers present and there were no concerns related to the questions being perceived as particularly confrontational in any way. Notes were written during the interviews in order to grasp the main elements that emerged during the interviews, and more detailed notes were written up as soon as it was possible. An interview guide was used to guarantee that all the main aspects of our study were addressed. In all cases we guaranteed confidentiality in the data collected. The guide was articulated in three different sections: after asking general questions concerning the background, role and experience of the respondent, the first section was linked to audit team composition and included questions related to the criteria and policies to select the members of the teams; the second section was mainly dedicated to investigating team dynamics and included questions related to the internal organization and management of the team; finally, the third section referred to the performance measurement and control of the team, and included questions linked to how the performance of the team was assessed and controlled as well as to how the team members were rewarded.

In order to guarantee sufficient coverage and perspectives on the structure and functioning of audit teams, we interviewed members of the auditing firms of the Big 4: in particular, we secured the contribution by three partners (indicated as "P" in Table 6.1), three managers (indicated as "M" in Table 6.1), six seniors (indicated as "S" in Table 6.1) and two juniors (indicated as "J" in Table 6.1) operating in small and big offices, in various countries and of different genders.

The evidence collected was repeatedly analyzed, first, individually by each researcher, and then jointly by all researchers.

In order to guarantee the quality of the findings, the researchers checked that there were no contradictory statements by the interviewees and that the evidence used to support the arguments proposed was reliable. Initially a "thick description" of each interview was prepared and the various elements proposed were analyzed in light of the context in which they were presented. Then to ensure a rigorous and complete analysis of the evidence, an interview-specific summary was developed for each interview and is reported in Table 6.1. This allowed for easy comparison of the answers provided by the different respondents, to understand the points of contacts and differences emerged during the various interviews, and then to make sure that the different elements described by the interviewees were comprehensively considered and included in the findings of the work.

Findings

Audit team composition

With reference to audit team composition, the interviews highlighted that the most salient criteria is industry specialization, defined in different ways (e.g. some audit firms have three industry levels' specialization, while others more than ten). In some cases, audit firms strictly apply these criteria only to managers and partners in order to let juniors and seniors diversify their experience and thus enrich their knowledge. Geographical location of the client seems to be another critical aspect, especially for smaller audit firm offices. In addition, the auditee's dimension and complexity are considered, in particular in order to assign the proper number of auditors with the necessary level of experience to riskier clients or to auditees representing a potential threat to auditor reputation. Audit team composition also depends on the years of engagement: for example new clients typically require a higher number of juniors' and seniors' hours.

The audit firm also tries to guarantee team continuity to recurring clients, considering however physiological turnover of junior resources and rotation rules. In particular circumstances, a client may ask for removal of specific auditors at lower levels, after the first year of engagement. Finally, timing and team members' scheduling overlaps are considered in team composition.

Typically, for clients closing their financial statements on December 31, audit teams are defined within September/October. The audit partner normally selects the managers, while in some cases the latter may suggest the seniors.

Audit team dynamics

Different professional levels are in charge of specific activities, which are clearly defined and homogeneous across the audit firms interviewed.

A critical moment in defining the audit plan is represented by the so-called kick-off meeting, which seems to be common practice. In such a meeting, all team members are usually involved for new clients, whereas only higher levels take part for recurring clients.

Supervision takes place at all levels, where the higher one monitors the activities performed by the lower one. There is no common practice of daily/weekly audit team members' meetings during the engagement, although a final closing meeting is usually held at the end of the engagement, when the work performed during the entire engagement is reviewed and relevant audit issues are shared.

Overall, the team style seems to be hierarchical. Exceptions involve small offices or specific geographical contexts, and may be explained by different cultural orientations. However, despite the hierarchical approach, there is continuous communication inside the team and consultations with specialists in order to solve critical issues and to optimize work allocation. Specialists are used mainly for tax and IT areas. Outsourcing of operative tasks is becoming more and more common, but only for a limited number of scheduled activities.

Interaction between team members and the client employees is diffused. The audit partner is specifically in charge of managing the relation with the client's representatives.

Turnover is quite common at the lower professional levels (i.e. juniors and seniors).

Audit team performance measurement and control

The findings indicate that the performance of auditing teams is a multidimensional phenomenon. In particular, this refers to many different aspects, involving some quantitative elements such as the number of hours worked for a specific client, and qualitative elements, including the quality and compliance of the work done and some soft skills such as the ability to interact with the client and the problem-solving capability.

With reference to quality-threatening behaviours and their causes, some important new elements emerged from the analysis of the evidence and which are not emphasized in the literature. One phenomenon that has been mentioned in the interviews and that is problematic is to carry out some of the activities once the opinion has been issued, with related effects on their formalization. Another important behaviour is represented by the lack of formalization, in the sense that auditors focus more on the substance of the work, but neglect some procedural aspects related to recording the activities and the results that have been carried out. This is especially the case for small clients, where the possibility to be screened by external reviewers is more limited.

Respondents indicated also that the drivers of quality-threatening behaviours are related to lack of time to carry out all the activities that are scheduled and a related phenomenon of under-staffing. Apart from these aspects that were already reported in the literature additional aspects seem to be relevant: on the one hand, the lack of priorities, so that all the activities and areas are often considered at the same level, and, on the other hand, the lack of experience of the auditors, who are involved in complex activities even in the first years of their professional development. This is more severe in some cases if it is accompanied by a lack of proper mentoring in explaining the work that has to be carried out. In addition, another element that may have an impact on the behaviours of auditors is represented by the lack of motivation, especially because the promotion expectations have not been met. A further element, which can contribute to generating quality problems, is represented by the existence of conflicts among team members or with the clients. This may happen either for contrasting personalities, or because there are different views between the auditor and the client on a specific technical issue. An unexpected antecedent of quality-threatening behaviours is represented also by too many working papers especially in non-critical areas. These documents may lead to confusion and accumulation of unnecessary documentation.

What is perceived as particularly relevant in the functioning of auditing teams could be related to the willingness of superiors to dedicate time to explain the work to the more junior staff and the relevance of the different activities as well as their involvement in the decision-making process and participation in meetings.

Among the mechanisms that are put in place to prevent quality-threatening behaviours are the development of a professional ethic through continuous training and the existence of a hotline for unethical behaviours related to work.

Table 6.1 Evidence from the interviews

	Audit team composition	Audit team dynamics	Audit team performance measurement and control
P1	The composition of the team depends on the following variables: • Industry specialization, • Auditor experience, • Balance between continuity and new fresh eyes, • Timing, • Geographical location. Internal policies for hours' allocation: • Partners (4–7 per cent), • Managers (15–20 per cent), • Seniors (around 30 per cent), • Juniors (the remaining hours). This allocation depends on client's size and complexity. The client may ask for specific auditors in order to guarantee continuity. The tentative schedule for resource allocation to each client is normally completed in September. Auditors that leave the firm do so in the transition between junior and senior or between senior and manager positions.	The operating management of the team is carried out by managers and seniors. It is important that partner(s) and manager(s) visit the client with a certain regularity. The critical moment for the audit plan is represented by a kick-off meeting where all levels are involved in cases where the client is new, whereas only the higher levels are involved in cases where the client is known. The management is rather informal and there is a strong identification with the office. Specialists are used mainly for tax and IT areas and they normally interact with the clients.	There is a continuous review process between each level and the lower one. Formal evaluation of all engagements of each partner every two years and of each manager every three years. There is also a yearly system that starts with objective setting at the beginning of the year and is concluded with a self-assessment approved by the supervisor for each level. Too many working papers may be problematic in terms of coordination of the work and have a negative impact on audit quality, especially if they refer to non-critical areas. Bonuses are allocated from the senior level upwards, depending on the amount of hours charged complemented by additional qualitative criteria and may range between 15–35 per cent of the salary.

P2	The composition of the team depends on the following variables: • Managers and partners are allocated according to industry specialization, juniors and seniors are allocated so as to diversify their experience; • Company status (public vs private); • Timing. The size of the audit team is determined based on client's complexity and risk.	Audit team dynamics depend on engagement complexity, where the higher the complexity, the more frequent and formal are audit team meetings. Multinational clients may imply multinational audit teams. The responsible audit partner periodically travels around sub-audit teams located in different countries. Specialists are used mainly for actuarial, financial instruments, taxes and forensic analysis.	Audit engagements are subject to periodical peer review procedures.
P3	The composition of the team depends on the following variables: • Industry specialization, • Geographical location; • Diversity (in terms e.g. of gender, background); • Auditee dimension and status (large, big, listed and unlisted). In particular, for listed companies, the audit firm selects the "best" partners who therefore might be allocated regardless of the industry specialization; • Audit firm tenure (e.g. new clients require a higher number of seniors' and juniors' hours). Team selection process starts at the partner level, who selects managers; the latter selects the seniors.	The critical moment for the audit plan is represented by a kick-off meeting. Management style is not hierarchical for cultural reasons. Internal conflicts that may arise during the engagement should be solved within the team.	Personal tutoring is provided by higher professional roles to immediate subordinates. Bonuses are assigned also at junior levels. Audit teams are subject to periodical internal review. Automation of standard procedures is an effective way to enhance audit team performance. Dispersion of auditors across too many engagements represents a threat on audit performance.

(Continued)

Table 6.1 (Continued)

	Audit team composition	Audit team dynamics	Audit team performance measurement and control
M1	The composition of the team depends on: • Dimension (if it is a group or not), • Complexity, • Geographical location, • Risks, • Industry specialization (for managers and partners). The higher the risk, the higher the proportion of hours allocated to expert auditors (e.g. public interest entities). The partner decides the manager to allocate to a specific engagement. The planning office matches the needs of all the other members of the team, paying particular attention to making sure that juniors have the possibility to work in different teams, so as to diversify their experience. There is usually low intervention by the managers on the resources preferred; it happens only in extraordinary and particularly complex cases. Engagements are usually opened in May and June and managers create the tables of the resources needed, then the planning office creates the final schedule around October.	Tasks of the professional roles: • Senior: guides the juniors and responsible for the review of the work, • Manager: planning; • Partner: general direction and coordination of the work. At the beginning of the activity, there is the team-planning event, directed by the partner and the manager at the presence of the entire team, also including the specialists. During the event there is discussion about the planning, the most important risks and other relevant audit issues. There is continuous supervision of the higher level on the lower one, also because they often work all together at the client office. If the client is small, the manager is present once or twice a week, if the client is big the manager is present every day. Specialist are primarily employed for corporate finance evaluations (especially impairment tests), retirement plans, derivative securities, taxes and forensic analysis. There is really little (< 5 per cent) outsourcing to an Indian company of the audit company for low-risk issues.	The critical elements for the audit team are: • Flexibility of the resources in their working hours and of the management in understanding personal needs, • Professional skepticism, • Proactivity, • Hard work. It is important to involve the resources in the entire process so that they can appreciate the value of their work. It is also important to improve soft-skills with the client.

For recurring clients, the team remains as similar as possible, considering rotation rules, employee changes of roles and a physiological change of the 20–25 per cent of the junior resources.

M2 The average team is composed of one partner, one manager, one senior and one or two juniors. The team of a big client might be composed of two partners (even if it is always only one who signs), one senior manager, one manager and many seniors and juniors.

Hours are allocated to each client on a risk basis. A common practice is the following:

- 5 per cent hours partner,
- 20–25 per cent manager,
- 40 per cent senior,
- 35 per cent junior.

The team composition depends on the industry; there is a particular distinction between the banking/assurance/SGR sectors and the manufacturing one. In the future, the idea is to have sub-industry levels within the manufacturing one.

Recurring clients may ask to have specific auditors (at all levels) allocated to the client for different reasons (e.g. team continuity, substitution of team members).

Rarely some external specialists are used for really specific matters, in those rare cases they maximize communication with the other auditors to share all information needed.

The work is divided into an interim phase and a final phase.

At the beginning there is a team planning event in which all the team is present, including the specialists, and they discuss the planning and the most important risks.

The senior is the most operative role, with high responsibility and high interaction with the client.

The management style is cooperative and horizontal. They use workspace in a flexible way, with no assigned offices for anyone, all the levels work together and they just sit where they find some space in the morning. Nevertheless, there is always high respect of seniority.

Colleagues develop great relationships with each other.

One of the main problems might be people dissatisfaction due to many reasons, such as for example in promotion delays.

Other conflicts may arise if the resources are arrogant, especially if they are young. Conflicts with the client regarding the technical issues are easier to solve than personal ones.

Every resource completes a weekly time report of the time spent.

Every level continuously reviews the lower one.

Critical elements for the audit team are:

- Respect of the seniority,
- Collaboration,
- Good and friendly environment.

There are internal reviews of the quality of the work done in order to ensure quality at the global level of the audit company.

All the team members receive an evaluation from the upper level for which they worked for more than 40 hours: if the evaluation is good the resource progresses to the upper career level, and if she or he is a senior or a manager receives a bonus. At the end of the year all the evaluations are collected and they are summed up in a rating (A, B, C). If the rating is A there is a progression. The items evaluated are the activities (especially timeliness and quality of the work), the relation with the client and the general awareness of the job.

Juniors are paid for extra hours, while seniors and managers are not, but they might receive the bonus.

(Continued)

Table 6.1 (Continued)

	Audit team composition	Audit team dynamics	Audit team performance measurement and control
	There is also a particular distinction for clients listed in the US, because the resources at all levels must have training for the PCAOB requirements. There is a tendency to keep similar the team of a recurring engagement. Senior and junior resources are allocated by the planning department, while managers are decided by the planning department together with the partners. The best resources at every level are allocated to the most important listed clients. This is also considered a rewarding mechanism for the best auditors.	In the case of contrasting personalities of two team members, the member occupying the lower level is removed. Specialists for taxes and IT are used in 85 per cent of the cases, more rarely specialists of evaluation and impairment test, real estate, transfer pricing. There is always great interaction between specialists and the audit team.	Resources have 60/70 compulsory hours a year of training for every level.
M3	Team composition is based on the distinction among manufacturing, and bank and insurance industries. The most important criterion for team composition is represented by the size of the client. There are no formal policies for gender team composition, but just a recommendation to have a gender balance.	Interaction between team members occur: • In one meeting at interim, • In one meeting at the final debriefing. Others may occur after fieldwork and before issuance of the report. The management prepares the report, which is approved by the partner. The partner approves also the strategies, the procedures and conclusions.	The under-reporting of time was worse in the past. Under-reporting of time is for extra hours but teams try to avoid extra hours. Senior associates and managers are evaluated on the basis of hours. Actual hours are always above the budget, but under-reporting of time keeps it to a minimum.

Clients do not react very well to changes in team members and require explanation. If the client has a problem with one member of the team, he or she is normally replaced.

Managers tend to be constant members of the team. Rotation is only for partners.

The client doesn't want to have team members who are also operating for competitors for confidentiality reasons.

The typical organization of the team is:

* Partners (2 per cent),
* Managers (15 per cent),
* Field staff (83 per cent).

The manager decides the number of hours with a budget approved by the partner, leading to a fee proposed to the client.

The clients normally do not know the hours, they just know the fee. In some cases they may require the total hours and the average rate.

The specialists involved in the team are usually the IT, tax and finance experts. Sometimes the specialist is not planned at the beginning of the engagement.

In important meetings, normally the partner and the manager participate together with the CFO of the client and the financial manager.

In a year, the manager meets the partner six to seven times per year.

The partners have access to the audit files and can monitor whatever he or she wants. It's good to maintain hierarchy but it is not that important. All members have the same background but there are differences in terms of experience.

Auditors work well with a friendly atmosphere, without formality. Doors of managers are always open. Less formal communication. Jokes and coaching more than managing.

It is important to provide explanation of why the procedures have not been applied adequately.

The criteria for interaction are an open mind and readiness to listen.

The day-to-day operations are managed by the senior associate.

The contact with the client is through the manager.

Judgement is different in public companies and small companies, due to the difference in the risk of litigation.

The client exceptionally can pay more if a specific event occurred.

Senior associates do the fieldwork. Managers supervise and contribute in significant areas (high-risk areas such as impairment). Partners review the procedures, the working papers in significant areas and conclusions.

Performance evaluations relate:

* For trainees, associates and senior associates to quality controls, relationship with the client and team work,
* For managers to the same criteria plus additional sales coming from new clients, engagements.

Judgement depends on the risk profile of the partner. A risk-oriented partner does not require much evidence, documents and specialists.

Conflicts may emerge with reference to competencies of team members or transfer from a big client to a small client.

(Continued)

Table 6.1 (Continued)

	Audit team composition	Audit team dynamics	Audit team performance measurement and control
S1	The composition of the team depends on the availability of the resources. The teams for the financial industry are less organized than the manufacturing ones. Seniors usually remain the same for recurring engagements, while juniors change. The main driver for assigning hours is the billing rate, so they are assigned as much as possible to the juniors and less to higher levels.	The TPE (team planning event), usually held in November, defines the audit strategies, the main risks and the need for specialists. Tasks of the professional roles: • Junior: routine works; • Senior: organizing timing and work; • Manager: network with the client and most complicated issues; • Partner: extremely complicated event and signature. There is constant everyday interaction between all the team members, and usually a meeting at the end of the week.	The number of hours spent are monitored to check the consistency with the expected ones. Bonuses are assigned based on both the audit company performance and the personal rating, which is, in turn, based on the work quality, the team management and the relationship with clients. Some conflicts arise for motivational reasons related to promotion delays.
S2	The composition of the team depends on auditee size and auditor's expertise. The minimum number of team members required is a manager, a partner and an operative person (either a senior or a junior appointed as senior for that engagement). There is a tendency to keep the same team members over the length of the engagement in order to protect client specific knowledge.	The manager plans the number of hours assigned to each member for the entire year at the beginning of October. Tasks of the professional roles: • Junior: first level analysis; • Senior: analyzes the documents obtained; • Manager: deals with the planning and analyzes parts of the financial statement related to the riskiest areas. Moreover, the manager plans the hours assigned; • Partner: signs the final report.	There is continuous informal monitoring of each member by the higher levels. The team outputs are measured through the client informal feedback and the AQR (quality reviews), performed yearly on a sample. At the end of the year everybody receives an evaluation, while juniors are also evaluated quarterly. The judgement is based on competencies, importance of the clients and strong personality. The evaluation is based on five questions to which it is possible to answer from "strongly disagree" to "strongly agree".

The planning function selects the team members randomly, but every level can informally express a preference on whom to be assigned at the lower level.

The client may ask for a specific partner or manager starting from the beginning of the engagement, and may suggest lower level auditors after the second year.

Before October, the team is defined and should meet.

If there is some tension between two members or with the client, the manager removes the member creating troubles, but usually after the end of September.

Outsourcing to the Indian service GTH (global talent hub) is used for operational tasks (and always for less than 10 per cent of the work). GTH does not interact with clients.

The seniors plan the work for the entire week on Monday, assign the activities to the juniors and checks what has been done.

Specialists of taxes are always used, while specialists of IT are used only for big clients.

Specialists are used for the tax area, for the IT area (especially for banks) and for the corporate finance (especially for private equity funds), and they often interact with larger clients.

Judgements might be restated due to the partner influence or the absence of enough space for people to progress, especially in peripheral offices.

There are whistle-blowing mechanisms thanks to the evaluations of every member, the partially variable wage of managers and seniors, and the motivation of the member.

Bonuses are allocated also to juniors and part of the salary of seniors and upper levels is variable based on performances, starting from 10–20 per cent of the gross salary.

Critical elements for the audit team are:
- Clarity of the work,
- Communication,
- Honesty.

The managerial style is horizontal and cooperative.

The higher the trust in the lower level, the higher the delegation.

Some conflicts might arise when expectations of upper levels are not respected, either because the upper level doesn't explain properly the task or because the lower level is actually not able to do the job.

(Continued)

Table 6.1 (Continued)

	Audit team composition	Audit team dynamics	Audit team performance measurement and control
S3	The composition of the team depends on: • Client size, • Client industry, • Audit team members' seniority. Educational background and gender of team members are absolutely random. SME's teams are composed of two juniors, one of whom with two years of experience, a senior, a manager, and a partner. For the first year engagements, the seniors and the managers are chosen on the basis of the industry specialization, while juniors are chosen randomly. For recurring engagements, an audit firm tries to ensure team continuity. The client has no influence on the team composition during the first year, but can subsequently ask for the removal of juniors and seniors. The formal deadline for the team definition is the beginning of October but it is usually defined even earlier.	The first years of the engagements the managers and the seniors are more involved in the audit activity, the following years the activities become easier and routine kicks in, unless extraordinary activities are carried out by the client. There are no morning meetings, but there is at least once a week a check of the activities performed. It depends on the single team and senior style. The activities are usually individual but examples of group activities can be the inventory and the analysis of a new area, when the juniors work with the seniors. The interaction with the client is usually daily but it is organized line by line (each level of the audit team interacts with the corresponding level of the client company). On the contrary the meetings with the senior management are planned in advance. Removals of team members might be caused by: • Request of one member to change industry, • Conflicts between two resources (if at the same level the one who started the argument is removed, unless he or she has a clear motivation),	There is a continuous informal monitoring of each member by the higher levels. At the end of the activity there is a formal monitoring of the output, which must be approved by the higher levels on e-audit (the audit company's audit platform). The immediate higher level has to motivate the subordinated role (i.e. by showing him or her a new area of the financial statements or letting him or her do interesting analyses rather than a routine one). The critical elements for the audit team are: • Good planning, • Flexibility, • Good interaction among team members. The style is usually hierarchical. Everybody refers to everybody else, but a certain order has to be respected. There is a quality control system within the audit company that randomly selects about one-third of the engagements. At the end of the control process, any weakness, if any, is detected and communicated to the related teams. This is a way to measure the outputs as well as to enhance the performances of the teams.

- The client requests the removal,
- The resource is not technically able to perform the task assigned,
- A love "affair" between two team members,
- Turnover.

Outsourcing is used for operative and routine activities up to 5 per cent of the hours dedicated to the engagement.

Specialists are involved for tax, IT and IRM (information risk management) during the first year. Audit specialists are involved in following years if deemed necessary.

The client gives its feedback about the professionalism shown by the team members (e.g. politeness, technical skills, efficiency). The feedback is structured and standardized in all countries of the world only for multinational clients, otherwise it is informal.

The quality can be undermined if:

- Any team member does not do the tasks properly (i.e. works very slowly or does not pay enough attention),
- There are conflicts among the members, so that the work environment is ruined.

The main whistle-blowing mechanism is the engagement review, which is a self-evaluation of team members of their personal strengths and weaknesses, for all engagements worked for more than 40 hours. The engagement review is followed by the year-end review to be filled by 15th July, in which the member assigns himself or herself a score from one to four. The immediate higher level can either approve or modify the self-evaluation, and the whole process determines a possible promotion or bonus. If the hours used to complete the activities are less than the ones agreed in the contract, the latter can be renegotiated the following year or the audit company

(Continued)

Table 6.1 (Continued)

	Audit team composition	Audit team dynamics	Audit team performance measurement and control
			can choose to underprice the service for a company and allocate less hours than the ones actually needed in order to get the control of a business or to penetrate a new market (strategic choice). The overtime is not usually included in the payroll, especially for the juniors, whose turnover is therefore affected.
S4	The minimum team size is one resource for each professional role, and the composition of the team depends on: • Size, • Industry, • Geographical location, • Auditor expertise, • The PCAOB accreditation (obtained attending a course) for the PCAOB engagements, • Independence of the team members, • Client risk. The planning function is responsible for the selection of the team members, but the manager can informally ask to work with a specific senior. The client does not have any role in the team composition, but at the end of the first engagement year, it can informally ask to remove a team member.	During the preliminary phase, the partner and the manager meet the rest of the team to define the inherent risk and control risk of the client company. Then, the manager and the senior decide which areas of the financial statements are riskier. The planning phase follows: the manager assigns the different activities within the perimeter of the scope. The seniors and the juniors are responsible for the operative activities. Finally, the partner signs the opinion. For recurring engagements, a higher proportion of activities are delegated to the lower levels, excluding the most relevant items (i.e. the manager will always be responsible for the impairment). Reasons for the change of the team members are: • Turnover,	The monitoring is continuous, unless there are imminent deadlines, in which case the activities are checked at the end of the week. The critical elements for the audit team are: • Good team building, • Trust, • Delegation of activities, • Providing support to lower levels if needed, • Communication, • Knowledge of the team members, • Presence of the manager. The output is measured based on the capacity of meeting deadlines and on the quality of the work. There are quality reviews of all the biggest client companies, at least one engagement per partner and one per manager and few random small companies.

There is a minimum number of hours that must be assigned to each professional role for each engagement; the higher the level, the lower the number of hours assigned.

- Conflicts,
- Overlaps.

The senior divides the activities among the team members and he or she organizes several informal morning meetings during the week.

The activities are individual and divided according to the financial statement areas. The interaction with the client is diffused. There is a continuous communication to solve eventual doubts or to understand how much work is left.

There is some outsourcing of operative tasks to an office in Albania for about 15 per cent of engagement hours.

Specialists are used almost always for the IT, sometimes for taxes, in case of acquisitions and for the impairment test.

Threatening behaviors are:

- Lack of motivation,
- Low focus on the work.

If the number of hours assigned isn't sufficient it is reported to the manager, who should increase the hours of the budget. If the manager thinks that he or she can't increase the fees, it is not possible to report any additional hours. Moreover, seniors and upper levels can't report any extra hours.

Single members' evaluation is divided into two phases: the preliminary one, in December, and the final one in May. In both sessions each assistant is evaluated first by the upper level, and then by the second higher hierarchical level. The evaluation is based on a scale from 1 (the lowest grade) to 5. The minimum grade to be promoted to the upper career level is 2, which is also the minimum grade for the seniors and the managers to obtain a bonus. The judgement is made on the basis of both soft skills with the client and the other team members, and hard skills of the work quality.

The style is hierarchical and everybody usually refers to the immediate upper level. Conflicts are usually due to conflicting personalities or low performance of one member.

(Continued)

Table 6.1 (Continued)

	Audit team composition	Audit team dynamics	Audit team performance measurement and control
S5	The composition of the team depends on: • Size, • Complexity, • The probability that the partner will be internally reviewed (if the probability is high, the best resources will be allocated to that team). The rule for the team members' selection is that seniors and juniors with previous experience with the client are chosen first and all the other members are appointed by the planning function.	Tasks of the professional roles: • Senior: manages the juniors and collaborates more and more with the manager in the planning, because he or she is more aware of some practical needs; • Manager: defines hours and fees with the client and is responsible for the planning; • Partner: gives guidelines and manages network with the client. The deliverables (final compulsory documents with the conclusions of the audit) are reviewed by the managers but also by the seniors if the client is small. There is a weekly planning for the activities of every day, more or less strict depending on the junior expertise.	The extremely common short deadlines maximize the incentive to be efficient and to focus the attention on the most important aspects. The critical elements for the audit team are: • Good soft skills and good technical knowledge, • Being proactive and good English, • Transparency in the communication. Every person is formally evaluated by his or her superior with a new system based on five parameters valued from one to four (strongly agree to strongly disagree) and one qualitative question for best and worst aspects of the person. All these reviews for each person are collected by one counselor, who has a major role in the evaluation discussion with her or his peers. This discussion defines the bonuses or promotions. The formal evaluation of seniors is based exclusively on the manager's perception, though the evaluation of the managers is more based on measurable results: the engagement efficiency and revenue generation.

S6

Minimum size of the team is one resource for each role. The team composition depends on:
- Auditor competencies,
- Client size,
- Distance of the auditor's home to the client company.

For recurring clients, the team composition is kept as similar as possible.

The planning function is responsible for the selection of the team members, but the manager can ask to work with a specific senior.

The client doesn't play any role in the initial composition of the team, but it can ask for the removal of certain members after the first year.

Team composition is usually planned in September.

Tasks of the professional roles:
- Juniors and seniors: control the single items of the financial statements and they deal with the operational tasks;
- Managers: responsible for the economic part of the engagement (invoices to the client, management of the fee), he or she has a representative role of the team;
- Partner: represents the audit company and he or she signs the final report and deals with complicated and extraordinary items.

Main determinants of team change:
- Turnover,
- Overlapping;
- Long distance from the client,
- The client doesn't like a member,
- Conflicts within the team.

The senior delegates the activities to the lower level and he or she usually checks the work progress once a week. There are no formal meetings but a continuous communication within the team.

The activities are individual, but the immediate higher level initially explains the task and he or she reviews the output.

The evaluation process is not perceived to be fair or transparent and that's one of the main reasons why people resign.

Possible threatening behaviors to the team:
- Criticism without real foundation,
- Not explaining guidelines properly.

The hierarchical structure of the company is important and influent in the relations.

The upper level must organize and manage the work properly in order to enhance the team performances. He or she must also be motivated and be able to transmit his or her passion to the lower levels.

The critical elements for the audit team are:
- Organization,
- Efficiency,
- Compatible personalities,
- Motivation,
- Cooperation.

There is an informal client feedback.

There is an internal "quality review" on a random sample of companies.

There might be checks performed by external authorities such as the CONSOB.

The manager is responsible for the economic part of the engagement and he or she decides how many hours to assign to each role.

Under-reporting of time used to be normal, but this year the practice has changed because lower levels don't need the manager's authorization to report extra hours anymore.

(Continued)

Table 6.1 (Continued)

	Audit team composition	Audit team dynamics	Audit team performance measurement and control
		Interaction with the client is diffused and individual, when performing single tasks.	Risk factors:
		Possible reasons of conflicts:	• Lack of time,
		• The lower level wastes time,	• Hostile environment,
		• He or she isn't motivated,	• Too much delegation to the lower levels without explaining the activities,
		• He or she has a difficult personality,	• Contrasting personalities,
		• The higher level delegates too many activities without explaining how to perform them.	• Lack of motivation.
		Outsourcing is used for 10–20 per cent of the work, to an office located in Albania, and is usually related to operative and mechanical tasks.	There is a biannual formal evaluation, based on a score (0 is the lowest and 5 the highest), which is determinant for the promotion to the upper career level as well as potential rewards. A 2.5 or a higher grade entitles to the variable portion of the salary.
		Specialist involved are generally IT and tax ones.	The judgement is affected by:
			• Competences,
			• Ability to interact with other people,
			• Efficiency.
			There is continuous review of the upper level on the lower one.
			The style is highly hierarchical with every level referring to the immediate upper level role, except for rare cases.
J1	Minimum size of the team is a person for each professional role. The team composition depends on:	At the beginning of the work, there is the kick-off meeting, in which all the team members meet and discuss the audit approach, the significant risks and procedures.	There is a continuous informal monitoring of each member on the lower level, and a formal review of the activity by the higher level at the end of the engagement.
	• Auditor's competencies,		There is an additional formal evaluation of
	• Client size.		

The partners and the planning function are responsible for the selection of the team members.

The client may informally ask for the removal of a team member.

The manager is appointed as soon as the new client is acquired; all the other members should be formally appointed by the beginning of October, but they are, in practice, appointed the day the team starts working for the client.

For recurring clients, audit firms try to maintain the same team members.

There are no morning meetings, but there is a constant communication among the team members and an ongoing control. For example if the senior is not present, the junior sends an email at the end of the day to recap the activities completed.

The style is very hierarchical, but changes according to the team.

The activities are individual, but there is cooperation within the team at the beginning and at the end of the activity.

The interaction with the client is daily and diffused.

For recurring engagements, everybody tends to delegate more.

There are specialists for tax, legal, IT, and corporate issues (e.g. derivatives or PPE valued at fair value). The level of involvement is quite high, but it's decreasing over the years of the engagement (even if it won't disappear).

There is outsourcing to the delivery center, which mainly deals with circularization or with other operative tasks, always for less than 5 per cent of the work.

The critical factors for the team are:
- Communication,
- Trust,
- Motivation.

The team output is measured through the client's formal feedback and the quality reviews performed by the partners of other offices of the audit company.

They are performed randomly on 20 per cent of the engagements. The aim is to foster the respect of internal policies and procedures, especially after the first year of engagement, when the teams tend to formalize documents less carefully.

One risk factor is the presence of slow unmotivated people that delay activities.

The activities-database, accessible to the entire team, is a whistle-blowing mechanism because it is possible to see who works slowly and to review the lower level, once every activity is completed.

For a big client the hours budgeted are usually enough, while for a small client often they are not. In this case the managers decide if charging the extra hours to the client or not, in general they don't want the client to pay fees much higher than the ones agreed upon.

(Continued)

Table 6.1 (Continued)

	Audit team composition	Audit team dynamics	Audit team performance measurement and control
J2	The team is composed on the basis of the client's industry. Usually the senior and the manager will arrange staffing for the team. The H&R manager in the department will also be involved in scheduling in order to avoid overlaps. Managers are selected by the partners and they are usually the same reported in the initial offer. During the audit tendering process or in debrief meetings, clients may ask for more resources at manager, senior, and junior levels.	There is a planning meeting, during which the manager and the partner decide how to approach the audit and create a budget for the number of hours of each grade required. The partner and the manager focus on the client management. The managers work also on the more difficult and technical areas of the audit. Senior auditors and juniors are mostly responsible for executing tasks. The team might change during the engagement due to: • Overlap, • Leave, • Training. Management is hierarchical; there is a lot of vertical delegation. Anyway, there is also some horizontal delegation to manage the workload between members.	Performance depends on the planning and organizing capabilities of the senior and on whether the team members suit each other, so whether they create synergies. The critical factors for the team are: • Organization, • Team work, • Communication, • Good team environment. The most threatening factors are laziness and bad technical knowledge. There is a whistle-blowing hotline for unethical actions relating to work. The client gives informal feedback at the end of the engagement, with comments for the next year. After an audit is complete, there is a debrief session, where the upper level appraises the lower level work. There are also performance appraisals every six months.

Activities and tasks are usually assigned to individuals.

Interaction with the client is usually common at all levels, but with some particular clients the resources collect the queries and the senior clarifies them in a formal meeting.

There is some outsourcing to an Indian company controlled by the audit company, for some junior-level tasks.

There are specialists for tax, consulting, IT, and pensions.

Generally, there is a push to report time correctly, and if it is suspected that hours are under-reported the resource manager will investigate this. If it is determined that hours have been under-reported, they will be corrected, but there isn't any disciplinary action as generally less hours look better for the managers.

Engagements have to be as profitable as possible, therefore they tend to be understaffed.

There is also a system where managers can award days off or cash vouchers to spend. Performance is also important for the annual raise discussion.

One of the risks perceived by the respondents is that some auditors could receive offers from their clients and may decide to leave the audit company. The involvement, team identity and good organizational atmosphere seem to prevent this phenomenon from happening.

According to the evidence, the evaluation system is hierarchical and based on the principle that each auditor receives an evaluation by the upper levels who worked with her or him. The junior staff are evaluated on the basis of various dimensions, with reference to which the upper levels have to express an assessment, and then the performance is compared with that of the other junior staff. This evaluation is mainly used for promotions. For seniors and managers the process is exactly the same, except for the specific objectives that are assigned to them. The evaluation is provided for each engagement. One of the issues is related to the fact that for seniors, what matters is just the perception of the managers and there are no objective indicators. On the contrary, managers have more measurable objectives related to the number of hours charged to the client, the revenues generated, and so on. To complete the evaluation process, each member of the firm has a counselor who collects all the evaluations of a certain member and meets with the other counselors of the same professional level to express a comprehensive evaluation that needs to meet a normal distribution, given that the result of this evaluation is used for assigning the variable part of the compensation. The main aspects that are considered are related to quality of the work done, interaction with the client, and teamwork. One issue that is reported with reference to this entire process is related to the lack of transparency and the political and power dynamics that affect the entire process more than meritocracy.

Appendix – checklist interviews

Audit team composition

What are the general criteria for defining the team composition? (industry vs geographical areas; homogeneous composition or diversification in terms of competencies, gender, background-education)

Are there policies for team composition (in terms of gender, rotation, apart from those that are regulated by law or regulators)?

Who is involved in the selection of the members of the auditing teams in charge of specific clients? Are there constraints, and what are they?

What is the role of the client in the initial team composition and adaptation during the engagement?

What are the criteria for assigning hours to the different levels? Is there under-reporting of timing and how is it dealt with?

What is the role (client management, tasks management, tasks execution) of the various professional roles (partner, manager, senior) and how does it change over the life cycle of the engagement?

What is the level and role of outsourcing?

What is the role and level of involvement of specialists?

What are the interfaces between the outsourcing members and the specialists?

What is the timing for team definition?

What is the level of change or adaptation of the team and the related determinants during the engagement?

Audit team dynamics

What is the internal organization of the team? (who does what? morning meetings?)

What is the style of management? (hierarchical vs horizontal, e.g. is every level referring just to the immediate higher level? Individual vs group activities)? What are the modes of interaction with the client (centralized vs diffused)? Are there daily meetings? How is the monitoring organized? (continuous or output?)

Do you think that there are preferred modalities to enhance performance and do you think that these previously listed elements are just team-specific?

What are, in your view, the critical elements that make the audit team work effectively?

Audit team performance measurement and control

How are the team outputs measured?

How is the team effectiveness measured and what are the potential quality-threatening behaviours and the risk factors? Are there any whistle-blowing mechanisms?

How are the team members evaluated and rewarded?

Do you have examples of a member removal from the team? Why?

Do you have examples of conflicts activated in the teams? What are the reasons?

What are the elements that affect the judgement?

Are there cases that would have led to judgement restatements? Which were the reasons for that?

What are the criteria for the internal audit of the auditing teams?

7 Conclusions

In this book, we have presented a review of the literature related to the management of audit firms, centred around the role, characteristics, and dynamics of auditing teams. This review, which draws from key contributions in the areas of psychology, organization, auditing, and management accounting, is selective and illustrative of issues pertinent to the understanding of auditing teams and does not attempt a comprehensive coverage of relevant research on the topic. We have also reported the results of a qualitative analysis of data collected from semi-structured interviews in the field to complement theoretical foundations with the "voice" of the practice.

In this final chapter, we will bring together some theoretical as well as some managerial takeaways that emerge from our work and which summarize the key points that in our view researchers and professionals should consider when approaching audit teams. In what follows, we report our conclusions according to the logic path that has been used across the chapters of the book.

- Recognizing that audit firms are professional and knowledge-intensive firms has implications in terms of how they are organized and managed. The organizational structure tends to be flat because the coordination and control of activities are carried out directly by professionals. In addition, there is a need to achieve a balance between professional norms and organizational values (Hinings, Brown, and Greenwood 1991; Starbuck 1992; Winch and Schneider 1993; Von Nordenflycht 2010). Moreover, complex organizational dynamics related to the generation and transfer of knowledge require the introduction of suitable knowledge management strategies, which affect how professionals act within the firm (Morris and Empson 1998). Finally, specific performance metrics that grasp the effectiveness and productivity of individuals are needed (Barber and Strack 2005).
- The management of audit firms requires a balance between the market of professional services and the market for professional workforce, on

the one hand, and the firm's economic and organizational structures, on the other. These four elements are in equilibrium in a way that changes in one of these elements have implications on the other elements (Maister 1982, 1993). So it is important for the audit firms to recognize those variables that can be hardly controlled, like, for example the billing rates and the compensation rates, and focus more on those levers that can be acted upon, such as the project team structure (i.e. the average or typical proportion of time required from professionals at different levels) and the level of productivity of auditors.

- The way in which technocratic controls (i.e. manuals, work methodologies, career paths) interact and merge with socio-ideological modes of control (i.e. shared values, beliefs) in audit firms is a central dimension in their functioning (Alvesson and Kärreman 2004). In fact, technocratic controls concentrate on the behavioural level, but they produce also a socio-ideological influence – as they are a means for creating and maintaining shared understanding and shared meanings. They work efficiently when their messages find a receptive audience gradually formed by the control, delivery and feedback cultures. In the same way, socio-ideological forms of controls are important means in shaping the thinking, feeling, and organizational identity that support the technocratic structure. This interaction is essential, because if technocratic controls and socio-ideological controls are not aligned, but contradict each other, they can be a source of conflict and disorientation for individuals and be detrimental for the performance in the long run.
- As some of the relevant characteristics in explaining an auditor's performance are almost partially innate, and thus cannot be significantly changed over the auditor's life, they should be carefully considered in the selection of new entrants into the profession. At the same time, audit firms and professional bodies could undertake appropriate actions in order to reinforce other impactful individual attributes, such as auditor expertise as well as organizational and environmental conditions associated with better auditors' judgements and better audit outcomes.
- Individual auditors do not work in isolation and thus their behaviors are affected by interactions within the auditing teams in which they operate. Therefore, focusing only on individuals may be problematic, as suggested by the results of single-person studies which cannot be generalized to multi-person settings (Trotman, Bauer, and Humphreys 2015).
- The focus on audit team diversity, which is highlighted in the global reports, the audit quality reports, and the annual reviews of the Big 4 as one of the key drivers in audit team composition, does not seem to be particularly emphasized by the auditors interviewed. Also, the impact of audit team diversity on audit quality and audit activity in

general should be better analyzed by the audit literature, which has so far partly ignored the topic (one of the recent papers dealing with this issue is the work by Cameran, Ditillo, and Pettinicchio 2017).

- Audit firms should also consider employing alternative methods of brainstorming compared to the open/unstructured ones, which appear to be the most widely used in practice. More specifically, audit firms should consider introducing guidelines, premortem scenarios or using electronic support to conduct brainstorming sessions, given that these features seem to increase the frequency and quality of fraud ideas. This would permit auditors to optimize the use of brainstorming sessions, instead of merely complying with what is required by audit standards. Moreover, it is also interesting to notice that the use of brainstorming sessions during the audit engagement was not highlighted as one of the key aspects by the auditors interviewed.

- There is a general level of consensus about audit specialization playing a crucial role in increasing audit effectiveness both at the individual and team levels. This aspect seems to be well accepted by practice, with audit firms considering industry specialization as one of the key drivers of audit team composition. Audit firms are also increasing the level of audit specialization by considering sub-industry dimensions.

- A recent trend in the management of the review process, and more in general of some other bureaucratic controls, used by audit firms is a transformation from a diagnostic use of these controls to an interactive role. This means that the audit review process has changed from being primarily focused on the compliance with pre-specified procedures to being directed to any exceptional audit findings, with a high level of face-to-face discussion with the audit team and questioning of its work and outputs (Pierce and Sweeney 2005).

- Whereas in an audit firm market controls are adopted to define the overall targets for cost and quality goals, and bureaucratic controls are used extensively to guide and monitor the work of auditors at different levels, clan controls play an essential role because in these firms a lot of objectives are difficult to translate into explicit and verifiable performance measures. So clan controls allow to achieve a fit between the individuals and the organization, and an appropriate balance between trust relationships, mentoring, and monitoring (Pierce and Sweeney 2005). Furthermore, clan controls may act as important precautions against quality threatening behaviours.

- Some critical elements of audit firms' management emerging from the evidence collected from the field refer to the behaviours that may threaten the quality of the audit work and which are less related to the structural features of the control systems, as suggested by extant literature, and more to the soft dimensions of management, such as the lack of direction, lack of motivation, and existing conflicts between auditors within the team and with the client. With reference to the performance evaluation system, perceived dysfunctional aspects reported by the respondents are linked to the lack of transparency of this process and the political and power dynamics that affect the assessment of individuals rather than a pure focus on meritocracy.

Since this is an attempt to scratch the surface of such an important and multifaceted phenomenon, the hope is that the readers that have appreciated the insights presented in this book will contribute to further developing the issues herein, both in theory and practice, helping to deepen our knowledge by increasing reflections and empirical investigations on the topic.

References

Alvesson, M., and Kärreman, D. (2004) Interfaces of control: Technocratic and socio-ideological control in a global management consultancy firm. *Accounting, Organizations and Society*, *29*(3), 423–444.

Barber, F., and Strack, R. (2005) The surprising economics of a "people business". *Harvard Business Review*, *83*(6), 80–90.

Cameran M., A. Ditillo, and A. Pettinicchio Audit Team Attributes Matter: How diversity affects audit quality, *European Accounting Review*, forthcoming 2017.

Hinings, C. R., Brown, J. L., and Greenwood, R. (1991) Change in an autonomous professional organization. *Journal of Management Studies*, *28*(4), 375–393.

Maister, D. H. (1982) Balancing the professional service firm. *Sloan Management Review*, *24*(1), 15.

Maister, D. (1993) *Managing the professional firm*. New York: Free Press.

Morris, T., and Empson, L. (1998) Organisation and expertise: An exploration of knowledge bases and the management of accounting and consulting firms. *Accounting, Organizations and Society*, *23*(5), 609–624.

Pierce, B., and Sweeney, B. (2005) Management control in audit firms – partners' perspectives. *Management Accounting Research*, *16*(3), 340–370.

Starbuck, W. H. (1992) Learning by knowledge-intensive firms. *Journal of Management Studies*, *29*(6), 713–740.

Trotman, K. T., Bauer, T. D., and Humphreys, K. A. (2015) Group judgment and decision making in auditing: Past and future research. *Accounting, Organizations and Society*, *47*, 56–72.

Von Nordenflycht, A. (2010) What is a professional service firm? Toward a theory and taxonomy of knowledge-intensive firms. *Academy of Management Review*, *35*(1), 155–174.

Winch, G., and Schneider, E. (1993) Managing the knowledge-based organization: The case of architectural practice. *Journal of Management Studies*, *30*(6), 923–937.

Index

Page numbers in italics indicate tables.

For Product Safety Concerns and Information please contact our EU
representative GPSR@taylorandfrancis.com
Taylor & Francis Verlag GmbH, Kaufingerstraße 24, 80331 München, Germany